TURNING SOUTH:
CHRISTIAN SCHOLARS IN AN AGE
OF WORLD CHRISTIANITY

Joel Carpenter, *series editor*

The Turning South: Christian Scholars in an Age of World Christianity series offers reflections by eminent Christian scholars who have turned their attention and commitments toward the global South and East. In order to inspire and move the rising generation of Christian scholars in the Northern Hemisphere to engage the thought world and issues of the global South more vigorously, the series books highlight such reorientations and ask what the implications of "turning South" are for Christian thought and creativity in a variety of cultural fields.

Also available in the series

Journey toward Justice: Personal Encounters in the Global South
Nicholas P. Wolterstorff

I have spoken of your faithfulness.
—Psalm 40:10 (NRSV)

I cannot become myself without another.
—Mikhail Bakhtin

People are people through other people.
—African proverb

TURNING SOUTH

READING A
DIFFERENT STORY

A CHRISTIAN SCHOLAR'S JOURNEY
FROM AMERICA TO AFRICA

SUSAN VANZANTEN

Baker Academic

a division of Baker Publishing Group
Grand Rapids, Michigan

Published by Baker Academic
a division of Baker Publishing Group
P.O. Box 6287, Grand Rapids, MI 49516-6287
www.bakeracademic.com

Printed in the United States of America

Library of Congress Cataloging-in-Publication Data is on file at the Library of Congress, Washington, DC.

ISBN: 978-0-8010-3994-2

13 14 15 16 17 18 19   7 6 5 4 3 2 1

Contents

Series Preface

Nearly forty years ago, the Scottish church historian Andrew F. Walls predicted that Africa would become the new Christian heartland and that other regions to the global South and East would become the new main places in the world for Christian practice and thought. Few of Walls's colleagues paid him any attention then, but today we see how prophetic he was. The "coming of global Christianity," as historian Philip Jenkins put it, is gaining broad interest and attention, and its signs are quite evident. Africans have recently led the World Council of Churches and several of the Protestant world communions. The South African Nobel laureate Desmond Tutu is arguably the world's most prominent public theologian. China and Brazil are now closing in on the United States as having the world's largest national populations of Protestant Christians. And not only has the balance of Christianity's place in the world tipped markedly toward the global South and East, but so has public and scholarly consciousness of it.

This global shift in Christianity's demography, vitality, and influence has caught most Christian scholars in the North Atlantic region by surprise. Their orientation and sense of mandate has been toward the problems of the increasingly post-Christian West, and their preparation for dealing with these issues has been framed within the European "Christian humanist" tradition. C. S. Lewis, Abraham Kuyper, and Dorothy Sayers are their patron saints, and one of their prime mandates has been to try to take back intellectual territory from the "cultured despisers of religion." Christian scholarly guilds, colleges, and universities are deeply oriented in this direction. Their strategies and preoccupations were forged on the anvils of European Christendom. As a result, says Walls, there is a major mismatch between Christian vigor and engagement in frontline mission and Christian resources for producing scholarly work. Christian scholarship needs a major reorientation.

Walls took that idea to heart, and he set to work rewriting the church history syllabus. It needed to reflect the implications of the gospel's traveling south and east from Jerusalem as well as to the north and west. There are others too who have been reorienting their personal and scholarly callings, and the purpose of this series is to give several Christian thought leaders the opportunity to share what they have been learning. May these reflections be powerfully instructive, so that many of you who read and ponder them will turn your hearts, minds, and vocations in this new direction.

Series Editor's Foreword

JOEL CARPENTER

S usan VanZanten, who first earned her license as a literary scholar with a dissertation on *Moby-Dick*, says that turning to the global South and to African literature was itself a great voyage, taking her, like the whalers, from New England to South Africa and beyond. In this delightful memoir, Susan leads us from her childhood home in a small Dutch American Calvinist community through college and graduate school years and on into a long and fruitful career of teaching and learning in Christian liberal arts colleges.

Frequently we see Susan's dissatisfaction with the way that things are in these settings, but this is no typical narrative of self-discovery and artistic liberation. Rather, like the whalers on the hunt, she says, she was being driven in unexpected directions by winds that, as she looks back, were surprisingly providential. For example, Susan says that she became a feminist because of those "whip-smart, academically hungry, socially confused women students" who looked to her for guidance as the only woman professor at her first teaching post. And she first turned to South African literature, she says, because her college required students to get some exposure outside of the Euro-American West—and somebody had to help them do it. So the small-college burden of teaching beyond one's expertise providentially turned Susan's curiosity toward the global South. And given her Dutch Reformed upbringing and grad-school sojourn in the American South and Southern literature, she had some providentially planted sensibilities for understanding the uniquely South African imagination, so deeply marked by sin and suffering.

This is but the start of Susan's intellectual and spiritual journey. She also discovers the roles of artistry and justice seeking in God's grand purposes, how a worldwide range of literary study helps Christians fulfill the call to love their neighbors, and the religious blind spot in postcolonial theory. She shows too how American literature's preoccupation with the individual needs the counterbalance of African literature's testimony to the "power, compassion, and necessity" of communal relationships.

Susan reflects throughout on both the constraints and the opportunities of working within Christian academic communities. And in the end, she testifies that it is a worthy calling for young scholars who are disciples of Jesus Christ. But in an age of radical global interactivity, she insists, Christian learning needs to be aware of the ways in which a faith that is now firmly rooted in the global South tugs at us all. We need to refresh Christian scholarship in the global North, she says, and that renewal will come as we turn to the South. Especially for younger scholars exploring new intellectual pursuits, the possibilities entailed in making such a move are promising indeed. It is difficult for me to imagine a more compelling book than this one to call young Christian humanists to a life of reading, writing, thinking, and teaching.

❖ 1 ❖

Loomings

1955–78

In the American epic *Moby-Dick*, the monomaniacal Captain Ahab and a ragtag crew sail the globe in pursuit of the elusive white whale, embarking from Nantucket, turning south at the Azores, skirting the Cape of Good Hope, and traversing the Indian Ocean to confront their adversary in the Japanese cruising grounds of the Pacific. Some thirty years ago, I wrote my dissertation about this grand pursuit, and in the following decades, I unexpectedly found myself taking a similar journey, launching from New England and landing in South Africa, undertaking an intellectual voyage during which, like Melville's Ishmael, "I have swum through oceans and sailed through libraries," as well as soared through air and searched through archives.

Although my graduate training in the late 1970s was in classic nineteenth-century American literature (Hawthorne, Melville, Dickinson), for much of my professional life, my research has focused on African literature. My scholarly turn to the south was steered by a providential conjunction of personal circumstances, academic winds, and world events. One small opening led to an insignificant decision, which led to another opportunity, and so on. I've never operated with a five-year plan; rather, I've tried to be faithful to the opportunities and passions God has given me, the blue skies and my internal compass, and such attempts at faithfulness have taken me in unanticipated and sometimes ironic directions. My journey, like all journeys, was shaped by the cultural currents of its time.

In today's academic world, postcolonial literature programs include African texts; graduate students can specialize in numerous authors, areas, or genres of African literature; and monographs and essays on African literary topics are published by university presses and scholarly journals every year. But in 1982, when I finished my PhD and found myself an overwhelmed twenty-six-year-old assistant professor of English at a tiny Christian college, the only work of African literature I had ever read was Alan Paton's *Cry, the Beloved Country*. Given this modest beginning, people often ask me how I came to work on African literature, and herein lies the tale of this book, recounted in six chapters to which I've given titles from *Moby-Dick*—that profound quest to find one's vocation in the midst of an immense, beautiful, and bewildering world.

The first chapter of *Moby-Dick* is called "Loomings," and after a peerless opening—"Call me Ishmael"—the narrator points out humanity's seemingly inherent attraction to water, the way we are irresistibly drawn to pools, streams, lakes, and oceans to gaze into their depths or distances. "Meditation and water are wedded for ever," Ishmael says; we all see "the image of the ungraspable phantom of life" in the watery surface,[1] alternatively a mirror and a window, reflecting ourselves and revealing a previously unknown world. And so Ishmael sets off as a deckhand, a common sailor, acknowledging that his adventures play only a small role in a much larger story scripted by forces beyond himself: "And, doubtless, my going on this whaling voyage, formed part of the grand programme of Providence that was drawn up a long time ago. It came in as a sort of brief interlude and solo between more extensive performances."[2]

Only retrospectively does Ishmael see the hand of providence; initially he thought that going to sea "was a choice resulting from my

1. Herman Melville, *Moby-Dick; Or, The Whale* (Indianapolis: Bobbs-Merrill, 1964), 25, 26.
2. Ibid., 29.

own unbiased freewill and discriminating judgment," particularly his overwhelming curiosity about the "portentous and mysterious monster": the whale.[3] Ishmael's drive to find meaning, to discover truth, to understand mystery is a fascination that I share, but I also find myself participating in his retrospective insight. In reflecting on my intellectual voyage, a minor incident in the grander story of Christian scholarship, I can trace the outlines of the loving hand of providential care working with my subjective free will and fallible judgment to guide me on my voyage of discovery.

The Dutch American Subculture of Lynden

Like most American baby boomers, I grew up in a comfortable and sheltered environment, but my childhood world was even more restricted than that of most others of my generation. I was born and reared in Whatcom County, Washington, located in the northwestern corner of the United States, spread between the Cascade Mountains to the east and the Puget Sound to the west. The long, flat vistas of Whatcom County farmland extend under expansive blue or gray skies with churning clouds and are punctuated by the meandering Nooksack River, smaller streams and creeks, and the occasional lake or pond. To the east, emerald foothills blanketed with cedars, pines, and hemlocks crouch below the ten-thousand-foot snow-covered crags of Mount Baker, attended by the dual peaks of the Twin Sisters Mountain to the south. Whatcom County is one of the most quietly beautiful places on the earth.

My family and I lived on the outskirts of Lynden, a town about fifteen miles from the coast and five miles from the Canadian border. In 1960, when I was four, Lynden had a population of two thousand upright citizens and a handful of rascals, and it served as the commercial, educational, and religious center for the numerous Dutch American families whose dairy farms dotted the fertile Nooksack floodplain. When Lynden was first settled in the 1870s, the Scandinavian pioneers who encountered the indigenous peoples trekked

3. Ibid.

across the Oregon Trail or rode the Northern Pacific Railroad to Seattle before making their way up the coast by steamboat. Lynden was incorporated in 1891, with logging and sawmills its primary industries, but as the vast old-growth forests were harvested and the immense cedar stumps laboriously removed, agriculture took over.

Attracted by the mild climate, productive soil, and striking topographical resemblance to the flat farmlands of Holland (if one didn't look east), an influx of Dutch immigrants arrived at the turn of the century, journeying west from the farmlands of South Dakota, Iowa, and Michigan, where many had been unable to find land or employment after leaving the Netherlands. A second wave of Dutch arrived in Lynden directly from the mother country following World War I, with a third wave of immigration occurring after World War II, when dairy farmers from the northern province of Friesland left their war-scarred, economically depressed homeland. By the end of the 1950s, over half of Lynden's population was Dutch (with many more living on farms outside of town), and the "Hollanders," as the non-Dutch referred to them, formed what one Lynden historian calls "a society within a society," a tight ethnic enclave made up of a tangled web of family, old-country ties, Calvinist beliefs, and suspicions about American culture.[4]

As Lyndenites, we were proud of our heritage, and with little irony, nary a whiff of political correctness, and deliberately poor grammar, we would say, "If you ain't Dutch, you ain't much." Lynden had much to admire: wide tree-shaded streets, fastidiously manicured lawns, modest but spick-and-span homes, waves of spring daffodils and tulips, a profusion of churches, and a paucity of taverns. When I was in junior high, two anecdotes (still found today on the internet) captured the quiet, conservative, and orderly quintessence of Lynden. The first was that at one time Lynden held the world record for the most churches per square mile and per capita. The second was far more exciting to our adolescent sensibilities: Lynden had achieved international fame for its distinctive entrance. After turning east off the state highway, one drove into Lynden on Front Street, right through

4. Ed Nelson, *A History of Lynden* (Lynden: Lewis Publishing, 1995), 103. In the 2010 US Census, Lynden's population was almost twelve thousand.

the middle of the town cemetery. We fervently believed that Lynden had been featured in the popular syndicated newspaper comic *Ripley's Believe It or Not* as the only town in the world that one entered by driving through a graveyard.

The divided cemetery, however, symbolized a central fact of Lynden life: the paradoxical presence yet separation of a segment of the Dutch American community from the rest of Lynden. In 1857, the Dutch Reformed church in the United States had split into two groups—the older Reformed Church in America (RCA) and the newer Christian Reformed Church (CRC).[5] The RCA was more open to American culture, embraced English church services, and permitted membership in lodges such as the Elks or Masons. The CRC was more wary of "Americanization," maintained Dutch worship services into the 1960s, and prohibited involvement in fraternal orders. Since the Lynden Cemetery (on the south side of Front Street) had been founded by Freemasons and Odd Fellows, the Lynden CRC formed the Monumenta Cemetery Association in 1902 to purchase the land on the north side of Front Street.[6] One thus literally drove through the social and cultural divisions of Lynden when entering the town, with the CRC faithful buried on the left and the rest of the townspeople—Swedes, Norwegians, Catholics, RCA, and anyone else—interred on the right.

In my childhood, there were four CRC churches and one RCA church in Lynden. The CRC adherents unimaginatively named their churches First, Second, and Third CRC, until the population expanded to require a fourth house of worship in 1951, which some bold elders decided to call Bethel CRC. The fact that this was the church my family attended was one indication of our slightly progressive leanings. My two younger sisters and I also attended daily Vacation Bible School at the RCA church each summer (CRC churches didn't sponsor VBS—too American, too evangelical), but I suspect our presence was due more to my mother's need for a break than to an early familial ecumenism. The CRC highly valued education and intellectual activity, founding Christian schools and colleges, instilling a reverential respect for

5. The best history of Dutch America is found in James D. Bratt, *Dutch Calvinism in Modern America: A History of a Conservative Subculture* (Grand Rapids: Eerdmans, 1984).

6. Nelson, *History of Lynden*, 108–9.

ministers and teachers, and requiring rigorous catechetical instruction of its youth. A Christian school system had been established in Lynden by the earliest CRC contingent in 1910, and by the time I went to school, approximately half of the children in Lynden attended Lynden Christian, with the other half going to Lynden Public.

As I grew up in the 1960s—far from events unfolding in Woodstock, Berkeley, and Selma—my Lynden was Dutch and CRC. My father and grandfather spoke Dutch to each other, especially when they didn't want us to know what they were talking about, and a steady stream of towering, gangly Dutch cousins visited us over the years. I spent twelve years at Lynden Christian School and attended Bethel CRC for almost eighteen years. With the exception of a handful of neighbors, all of my childhood friends were Dutch and Christian Reformed.

Growing up in this robust ethnic subculture, I experienced a puzzling mixture of doctrine and piety, broad thought and narrow practices, cultural separation and cultural engagement. Historian James Bratt explains, "The Christian Reformed . . . prided themselves on strictness of creed and code."[7] The Bible was the central authoritative revelation, but the creeds, catechisms, and doctrinal formulations represented the best systematic articulation of biblical truth and were instilled at church, home, and school—the three mutually reinforcing realms of our lives. Bratt aptly sums up the mind-set that this training nurtured: "Faith became knowledge and that not an intuitive grasping but a rational assent to specific propositions. Religious feeling became secondary in the sequence of salvation, and so also in value and importance."[8] Head was more important than heart.

At Lynden Christian, I was taught the importance of an all-inclusive world-and-life view, the presuppositional foundations of all education, and the appositeness of faith for the full sweep of human life. But I also repeatedly encountered in my community a pietistic legalism and rejection of modern American culture, along with a call to separate from the secular realm. The CRC Christian world-and-life view critiqued the idolatry of modern American culture and constructed strict rules for life as a holy and separate people. This legalism, coupled

7. Bratt, *Dutch Calvinism*, 39–40.
8. Ibid., 134.

with old-country mores, led to strange juxtapositions that later in life I had difficulty explaining to my evangelical friends: children couldn't trick-or-treat on Halloween or play outdoor games on Sunday, but smoking was an acceptable practice for Dutch men (but not women). Gambling was strictly forbidden, but classical musical instruction was common in most families.

Bratt describes the Dutch American subculture of the 1940s as "a religious fortress," in which "appropriate strictures" were applied to "women's dress, popular songs, Freudian psychology, dancing, birth control (and the associated root evil of apartment living), divorce, and the movies."[9] Although Bratt is speaking of the 1940s, this fortress still closely guarded the Lynden of my childhood in the 1960s. Girls could not wear pants to school; rock and roll was a tool of the devil; all forms of dance were forbidden; I didn't know a single divorced person; and no one went to the movies. Freudian psychology and birth control weren't even on my radar screen, but I do think there were a few apartment buildings in Lynden. Only a few.

Family, Flowers, and Films

However, in my family life, there were subtle differences from this wider distrustful spirit of the Dutch American subculture. My paternal grandfather had immigrated to Lynden in 1931 to work for an American branch of the Dutch family bulb business, Gebroeders van Zanten. Following World War I, the United States banned imported bulbs, so rather than losing the profitable American market, Gebroeders van Zanten opened an American division. My grandfather's cousin ran the bulb side of the US business, while my grandfather built a greenhouse range to grow azaleas just a mile and a half from downtown Lynden. Van Zanten azaleas were hothouse plants, with dark green foliage and vivid red, pink, salmon, white, or picoteed flowers at their prime for Christmas and Valentine's Day.

My father spent his life growing azaleas, eventually taking over the business from my grandfather, so while most of my friends either

9. Ibid., 138.

lived on dairy farms or were "town kids" with parents who were store owners, teachers, or ministers, I grew up at what we simply called "the Greenhouses." This was a fifteen-acre complex of glass houses, a series of plastic "cloth houses," a grafting shed, a shipping shed, a cluttered shop, a pump house, and plentiful outdoor beds where three-year-old plants were transplanted for the summer before being shipped out across North America each fall. At the Greenhouses, my family lived in the small white house in which my father had grown up, surrounded by the rich odor of peat dirt, which we constantly tracked into the house, much to my mother's dismay.

My grandfather had moved to Bellingham, a small city about fifteen miles away, but he came to work every day and drank coffee in our kitchen at ten o'clock. Two of my uncles worked at the Greenhouses, and my bachelor uncle also lived at the Greenhouses in what we called "Shack #1," a dilapidated two-room structure attached to the shop. My maternal grandparents (Dutch CRC, of course) lived in Lynden, and we, along with a variety of aunts, uncles, and cousins, went to their house every Sunday after church for strong black coffee and lap lunches of ham buns, Jell-O salads, and homemade cookies. During the week, after piano lessons, I would walk to my grandparents' house where I did my homework until someone could drive to town to pick me up. My two younger sisters and I thus grew up surrounded, smothered, and sustained by family.

Tolstoy's celebrated opening sentence of *Anna Karenina* claims that "happy families are all alike; every unhappy family is unhappy in its own way," but we were a generally happy family that believed we were different from other Dutch CRC Lynden families. This unique identity was both a blessing and a curse. We were neither farm nor town, and while my grandfather was a man who worked in the dirt, I never once saw him (or my father) wear a pair of blue jeans or overalls. My grandfather was better educated than many Lyndenites, having studied French at the University of Grenoble. He read widely, loved art and music, and had a quiet, irrepressible, quirky humor. While most Lynden families came from the northern farming districts of Holland or Friesland, my paternal family's origins were in western Holland, in the bulb-growing areas near Haarlem. We were Dutch, no doubt, but we were different.

Although neither of my parents was a college graduate, they each had an ardent appreciation of literature, music, and theater, which they shared with their children. To my simultaneous admiration and frustration, they were completely unlike any of my friends' parents. They took their three daughters to the Oregon Shakespeare Festival every summer, were voracious and open-minded readers, and had season tickets to the Vancouver Opera. Lynden was only a forty-minute drive from Vancouver, British Columbia, and we went there regularly to attend children's concerts, visit the zoo and aquarium, picnic in Stanley Park, and, somewhat scandalously, go to the movies.

The CRC Synod did not declare movie attendance acceptable until 1966, and it took several more years before many Lyndenites would darken the door of a theater, but my parents had been going to movies for years—clandestinely while they were dating in high school. The first movie I remember seeing was Disney's *Babes in Toyland* (1961), with its terrifying account of two children lost in a woods. Three years later, we stood in what seemed like an endless line in a steady rain to see *Mary Poppins*, which I absolutely adored. I can still sing all the lyrics to the deliciously strident "Sister Suffragette."

We had long evening meals at home, at which we three girls debated a variety of issues with our parents while the tuna casserole congealed. Because we ate later than most of the neighborhood families, on long summer evenings, the neighborhood gang would gather outside our kitchen window impatiently waiting for my sister and me to come out to play Kick the Can or Any Annie Over. The neighborhood kids sat down at their family dinners at 5:00 and rose at 5:15. But the Van Zantens often were not finished until 7:00. I was torn—wanting to go out and play, yet longing to finesse my father in an argument.

Lynden life was almost exclusively concentrated on church, school, and home, and the most important topics of conversation concerned the weather, livestock, and high school sports. Sundays at my grand-parents' consisted of tedious discussions about the price of hay or corn, whose cousin married a boy from California, and whether the Vissers used to live on the Tromp Road or the King Tut Road. Occasionally the outside world broke in: when John F. Kennedy was shot, our school principal came into my first-grade classroom to inform the teacher, who stopped class to lead a prayer. Two years later my

mother took my sister and me out of school in order to see President
Lyndon B. Johnson sign the Columbia River Treaty at the Peace Arch
International Park in Blaine, another Whatcom County border town.
She thought we should have the opportunity to see our country's
president.

And I still remember watching Neil Armstrong step heavily into
the dust of the moon on July 20, 1969. It was a soft, warm, golden
evening, and I was at my weekly Sunday evening babysitting job car-
ing for the three little blonde-haired Stegink girls. After Mr. Stegink
picked me up, we listened to the radio coverage as we drove across
town. I was worried that I might miss seeing the actual moon walk,
but we finally arrived at the Steginks, where the girls were already in
bed. The Steginks left for evening church, seemingly unfazed at missing
history, and I rushed to turn on their tiny black-and-white portable
television just in time to watch the fuzzy picture and hear a scratchy
"That's one small step for a man, one giant leap for mankind." I was
thirteen years old, and I knew that the world had changed.

But for the most part, throughout grade school and junior high, the
tumultuous national and world events taking place outside Lynden—
the Cuban Missile Crisis, the Vietnam War, the antiwar movement,
the rise of feminism, the Six-Day War, the French student revolution
of 1968, the Civil Rights Act, even the assassination of Martin Luther
King Jr.—took place in a faraway land, a land that had little impact
on or relevance for me. No doubt some of this can be attributed to
childish self-absorption, but there also was a Lynden mentality that
we lived in a different world, a neat and orderly and honest world,
where diligence, frugality, and industriousness ruled, where women
made homes and food and clothing while men went to work and
disciplined the children and directed the church. The population of
Lynden was almost exclusively white and Western European, with a
few migrant Hispanic workers arriving in the summer to help harvest
the crops. There was one black man in town, named Joe, who worked
for a time at the greenhouses before becoming a cook for the highway
department, and I'm ashamed to admit that we called him "Black Joe."

As for my friends and me, besides the usual childhood games, alli-
ances, and betrayals, we were obsessed with sports. Lynden Christian
High School had a fierce rivalry with Lynden Public High School,

and the agonies of the muddy football season were followed by the ecstasies involved in the pursuit of the holy grail of the state basketball tournament. Unfortunately, to my social detriment, my parents had not the slightest interest in high school sports, and we never went to any games as a family.

However, we were faithful church members. I was a Calvinette—a Reformed Girl Scout who earned merit badges, wore a neck scarf, and attended summer camp—for a couple of years until I finally quit, but there was no rejecting years of catechism instruction, first on Tuesdays after school and later, in high school, on Wednesday nights. We worked our way through the fifty-two sections, or Lord's Days, of the Heidelberg Catechism, dutifully memorizing the questions and answers in archaic language to recite to our teacher.

Lord's Day 1

Question 1.
What is thy only comfort in life and death?

Answer.
That I with body and soul, both in life and death, am not my own, but belong unto my faithful Saviour Jesus Christ; who, with his precious blood, has fully satisfied for all my sins, and delivered me from all the power of the devil; and so preserves me that without the will of my heavenly Father, not a hair can fall from my head; yea, that all things must be subservient to my salvation, and therefore, by his Holy Spirit, He also assures me of eternal life, and makes me sincerely willing and ready, henceforth, to live unto him.

When I was younger, I had an almost photographic memory, so I could read each Lord's Day a couple of times before Catechism and repeat it perfectly. After the recitation, we took turns looking up and reading aloud the supporting biblical references. By the time I reached high school, the CRC had implemented a 1970s version of catechetical instruction, with hip contemporary language and elongated cartoon figures. As a teenager, I found this religious instruction excruciatingly dull, but in the years to come I discovered that my catechetical drills, combined with the thorough biblical education at my Christian school and dense doctrinal Sunday sermons, had irremediably steeped me in the language, metaphors, narratives, doctrine, and theology of the King James Bible and Reformed Christianity.

An Intellectual Hunger

The ability of rote instruction and tedious sermons to saturate and form my very being defies all learning theory, but I attribute their lasting imprint, in part, to the fact that an essential element of my identity was a passion for thought, an immense intellectual hunger that was valued by my Dutch immigrant community, although not always understood. When I was four, I often sat in my father's lap while he read the newspaper in a big red tweedy armchair. I'd scan the page for words that I knew, and then I would point to another word, intriguing because of its length or proximity to a picture, and ask, "What does that one say?" By the time I entered first grade, I was an adept reader, so I was dismayed when I was asked to sound out the words "See Spot Run. Run Spot Run" in *Fun with Dick and Jane*. Because I had already learned how to read by a process that I now know is called whole language acquisition, the combination of phonetics, simplistic prose, and inane stories frustrated me. I fear I was an unpleasant and rebellious child in first grade, but I can't remember exactly how I acted out, only that my wise mother eventually intervened and obtained permission for me to quietly read chapter books to myself when the rest of the class was having a reading lesson.

My father and I continued to read together, racing to see who could reach the end of the page first. I soon was outpacing him. Unconvinced that I was reading the entire text, my father would quiz me about the content, and he was pleasantly surprised to discover that my comprehension was excellent, despite the rapidity with which I read. (Years later, in graduate school, having to read a major text a day in order to make my way through my master's reading list in a summer, this speed-reading ability was an unforeseen blessing. I'm afraid that even I, however, faltered in the face of *Middlemarch* in one day.)

When I was in the sixth grade, my mother, who had finished two years at Calvin College before dropping out and getting married, began attending Western Washington State College in Bellingham in order to complete her degree. This was not what typical Lynden wives and mothers did, and the first day I left the school bus and entered an empty house, I unreasonably felt rejected. All my friends, I fretted, would find their mothers waiting for them, with milk and Toll House cookies, eager to ask about their day at school, but *I* had to supply the milk and cookies for myself and my sisters. When my mother came home, she was not interested in who got a new Barbie, the unfortunate softball incident at recess, or the cute dress Ann's mother was making. Instead, she and my father had long talks about the Russian history, American literature, or western geography she was studying.

At the time, I resented my mother's unconventional behavior; years later, I saw it in an entirely different light. She, too, was hungry. My mother was working on a library science degree, and when she enrolled for a course in children's literature, I became the class guinea pig, reading books she brought home, reporting on my reactions, answering specific questions posed by the class. I had strong opinions—some appreciative and some disparaging—about what I read and did not hesitate to articulate them. The seeds of my future life as an English professor and literary critic were being sown.

I was an insatiable and ubiquitous reader. I walked down the state highway once a month to plunder the county bookmobile, read dusty books about farm boys in the Midwest that were recommended by the Lynden town librarian, dutifully plowed through the mawkish Elsie Dinsmore volumes that the Bethel church librarian pressed upon me, and checked out ten books every Saturday at the Bellingham library. I read completely inappropriate books for my age, including *I Was Hitler's Doctor* (a shocking and eye-opening depiction of evil) and *Marjorie Morningstar* (a shocking and eye-opening depiction of sex). I was the classic kid with her nose constantly in a book, ignoring parental calls for dinner, responsibilities to watch my younger sisters, or orders to turn off my bedside light.

I read with a flashlight under the covers—ruining my eyes, according to my mother. I read in our living room with its wall-length custom-built bookcase crammed with books and phonograph records. I read in a secret cedar-tree hideaway, in the bathtub immersed in Mr. Bubble, and on the grass under the weeping willows down by the creek. Reading provided me with new worlds—whether fictional or historical—that were radically different from my dull life in a small farming community. For me, reading was an escape from Lynden.

So while I lived in a small, conservative, inwardly focused Dutch-immigrant town, my unconventional family and polymathic reading provided tantalizing glimpses of other worlds. Yet I had seen little of those worlds. Because my nurseryman father was always busy during the summer, our limited family vacations consisted of car camping in the Cascades, attending the Oregon Shakespeare Festival, and occasionally venturing to the California Redwoods or Oregon coast. The longest family trip we took was to the Canadian Rockies, and when I left home for college, I had seen nothing of the United States beyond the West Coast.

In high school, my intellectual hunger prompted a frenzy of activities. I joined the debate team and spent hours researching health care and pollution. I became a member of our newly established Ecology Club and marched to the Lynden dump on the first Earth Day in 1970. I edited the school newspaper and produced Lynden Christian's first underground paper, complete with rude comments about teachers that got me in trouble. Desperate to escape from Lynden, I applied to be an AFS (American Field Service) summer exchange student and was devastated when one of my best friends was selected instead of me. (This was before the days of church mission trips to Mexico or even farther fields.) I had a spiritual crisis and refused to make a profession of faith because, I claimed, the Christian Reformed Church was all head and no heart. I hung out at a local Christian coffeehouse, listened to Christian rock, and attended a charismatic Bible study. I went to a nondenominational church with my outsider boyfriend (not Dutch, not Lynden, not clean shaven). I had a bad case of Lynden fever.

Faith, Politics, and the Future

In the 1970s my parents became involved in county and state politics, with my father serving on the county planning commission and Republican precinct committee, and my mother helping to write a new county charter. (She eventually was elected to the Whatcom County

Council and in 1983 became the first woman county executive in the state of Washington.) Our dinnertime discussions turned increasingly to political issues, and I enrolled in a class called "World Problems," where I began to ponder the relationship between Christian faith and politics.

Until that point, my engagement with ideas was unselfconscious and unreflective, like a fish swimming in an ocean. I saw no dangers and experienced no struggles; my family (and some basic, at that time unrecognized, Reformed concepts) had instilled the confidence that the world belonged to God and that I was free to explore every part of it. In World Problems, we discussed current issues—the Paris Peace Talks, Nixon's visit to China, the IRA, and the Red Army—and were expected to articulate how our beliefs informed our views. For high school students who tended merely to repeat their parents' positions, this was challenging, and few were up to the task, especially the contingent of John Birchers who saw a communist behind every tree but were unable to articulate any reason for opposing an idea beyond the *c*-word. One friend and I delighted in arguing in favor of socialist positions, merely to stir up the John Birch boys, even though we were no advocates for communism ourselves. I learned much about circular reasoning and *ad hominem* arguments that term, as well as how to bring a variety of ideas—biblical, theological, political, and social—into fruitful synthesis.

During my senior year I was selected to attend a state conference for creative high school students held at Fort Worden, a late nineteenth-century fortification guarding the entrance to Puget Sound. Fort Worden had been converted into a state park, but the stark gray barracks, ornate Victorian officers' houses, and a warren of underground artillery bunkers still existed. Here I encountered the first real intellectual challenge to my worldview. Arguments about whether a Christian should dance or go to movies concerned interpretations of personal morality, I thought; questions of politics had to do with how one could most effectively apply Christ's teachings to solve the world's problems; questions of science were, for me, perhaps too easily resolved by a simple faith that scientific facts were accurate accounts of how the world functioned and that God was involved in some way in that process, even if I didn't understand exactly how.

But the Washington Creativity Conference dealt with anthropology and futurology, raising questions like, What is a person? What is self-awareness? Do we have any control over ourselves and our future? If so, how should that control be employed? How does creativity complement science?

We watched the film *Future Shock*, narrated by Orson Welles; we read Carl Rogers's "Freedom and Commitment"; and we sat in a solemn circle around the science-fiction writer Frank Herbert, who told us that the human mind had no limits, that we were the shapers of society's future, and who distributed bread and grape juice in an irreverent communion celebrating our creative powers. With a couple of other Christian students, I struggled to make sense of these experiences, sneaking out of the barracks at night to meet in a spider-ridden bunker to debrief by candlelight. The conference organizers' agenda was to convince us that we creative types were capable of influencing and informing our society's future just as much as the scientists; we, too, were the leaders of tomorrow.

The combination of earnest and wacky ideas, commitment to the common good, and grandiose self-perceptions troubled me, and over the course of the week, I became convinced that Christians, too, needed to be deliberately engaged in constructing the future. Christians needed to know and understand the world and its philosophy, culture, science, and technology in order to play a redeeming role. I didn't have much of a vocabulary or vision for what that redeeming role might consist of—that was to come much later—but I felt the first tug of conviction that my role in the world of ideas mattered to God.

When 120 students graduated from Lynden Christian High School in 1974, most remained in the area to get married, work on a farm or at a local business, or enroll in technical school. About twenty of us went to college, with the greatest number opting to follow a well-trod path to one of two Christian Reformed institutions: Calvin College in Grand Rapids, Michigan, for the more academic types, or Dordt College in Sioux Center, Iowa, for those wanting the familiar atmosphere of an agricultural town. Eager to escape Dutch Reformed country and to experience a more diverse Christian community, I did not apply to Calvin. As a high school senior I had visited the University of Washington, but one night in a raucous coed dorm and an hour in an Introduction to Psychology class of five hundred students convinced me that I wanted to go to a small, Christian liberal arts institution. My Lynden Christian years had taught me that there was no such thing as a purely objective education, and I wanted to learn from faculty who embraced Christian beliefs and were willing to take those ideas seriously. So I decided to attend Westmont, a nondenominational evangelical Christian college in the exclusive suburb of Montecito, outside of Santa Barbara, California. My family drove me to Sea-Tac Airport, and, teary and prematurely homesick, I boarded a Boeing jet and left them behind. It was the first time I had ever flown on a commercial airplane.

Christian Higher Education: Westmont College

Westmont was a perfect fit for me. I matriculated with a double major in political science and English, intending to become a journalist. After a year, I changed my mind; I now wanted to become a public defender or a legal aid society lawyer. I continued to pursue my double major, which would provide good preparation for law school, but I also worked for four years on the college newspaper, a weekly publication called the *Horizon*, becoming editor-in-chief during my senior year. My Westmont experience, both inside and outside the classroom, further fostered my commitment to social issues and to Christian higher education.

As the editor of the *Horizon*, I met weekly with the college president and the president of the Westmont College Student Association (WCSA), and navigated the highs and lows of campus politics. Every week saw a new outpouring of letters to the editor ranting or raving about the positions of our editorial team. We fought a running battle with the WCSA over what we believed to be their too-close ties with a campus service group called "Christian Concerns"; we expressed skepticism about the spiritual efficacy of the required chapel program; we had the audacity (according to our critics) to endorse a candidate in the WCSA presidential race. We expanded the paper's coverage of the arts; created a forum for more liberal students to advocate for, among other things, a food co-op, biblical feminism, and an increase in minority students; and put out a special issue on Potter's Clay—a newly created student mission trip to Ensenada, Mexico, over Easter break. (The Potter's Clay ministry continues today as "one of Westmont's longest-running traditions, and certainly its oldest, continuously-running ministry.")[10]

After the *Horizon* printed the *f*-word in a creative piece written by an eccentric campus arts activist who, along with another student, died in a head-on auto accident, I received a formal censure from the Westmont Publications Board. This was merely a rebuke—although if a second censure had occurred, I would have been removed as the editor—but I was devastated, even though I did not regret publishing the piece. At the end of my senior year, I wrote a farewell editorial advocating that more students get involved in campus life and cautioning, "Being a student leader is certainly a risk. I have gone through this difficult year being constantly dismayed and discouraged about this kind of role. At this point, I am too close to the situation to reflect fairly on it. However, I have the sneaking suspicion that in five or ten years I may look back on everything that has happened to me this year and realize the full value of it."[11] Three decades later, I can see that nothing prepared me so well for the constant struggles of academic life, both petty and profound, as that year at the helm of the *Horizon*.

I'm amazed, paging through the yellowing newsprint of my bound copy of that year's paper, by how many of the controversies in today's Christian college world were already present: one article discussed the difficulty of being a vegetarian on campus; an anonymous letter lamented the trials of being a homosexual at Westmont; a task force was convened to study the problem of minority student representation; a group of women formed a women's association and opened a women's center where you could check out *Our Bodies, Our Selves*. One headline announced, "Voskuyl Library Obtains Computer," the first hint of the impending revolution for a world in which electric typewriters were a coveted student possession.

The breadth of my own interests is also apparent. One week I wrote an editorial called "Be Activists of the '70s," calling on students to

10. See http://blogs.westmont.edu/potters-clay/about-2/.
11. "Senior Reflections: Concern with Apathy Expressed," *The Horizon*, May 5, 1978.

write then-Governor Jerry Brown to protest his veto of state scholarship monies "as a callous injustice harming primarily lower-income students." A few weeks later, I urged the virtue of academic pursuits: "I worry that often the emphasis on being a whole person comes only on the social aspect of that wholeness, to the neglect of the intellectual side. How often have you heard the argument, 'be a whole person, study!'?"

When a dynamic, popular philosophy professor, J. Randall Springer, announced that he was resigning his position at the end of the academic year, citing the "intellectual inadequacies of evangelicalism," I, along with many other students, wrestled with the implications. Was evangelicalism intellectually adequate? Coming from the Christian Reformed world, I had never faced this question before, and in lengthy lunchtime discussions with friends, I began to recognize the intellectual strength and consistency of a Reformed perspective that held that the sovereign God created the entire world, that Scripture was authoritative but not inerrant, and that using one's mind was a legitimate and significant way to serve God. In light of the evangelicalism of Westmont, parts of the Reformed tradition were beginning to take on a clearer focus.

Coupled with campus activism was my burgeoning engagement in the life of the mind. Westmont was full of smart and articulate people who thrived on thought. When the *Horizon* sponsored an essay-writing contest on the topic of "The Christian and Social Responsibility," I served as one of three judges, along with the dean of students and the infamous Professor Springer. Philip Clayton won, with an essay called "The Christian and Social Responsibility: Why Doesn't It Grab Us?" Second place went to Kevin Vanhoozer for "Pilgrim's Digress (A Fable in Three Social Acts)." Phil and Kevin were both philosophy majors, and the three of us had neighboring library cubicles that were allotted to honors students working on senior theses. All three of us became academics. Phil is now a professor of theology at Claremont School of Theology and describes himself as a panentheist defending a form of process theology that is hypothetical, dialogical, and pluralistic.[12] Kevin is a noted evangelical theologian with a strong interest

12. See http://www.cst.edu/academics/faculty/profile/philip-clayton/.

in hermeneutics and serves as the Research Professor of Systematic Theology at Trinity Evangelical Divinity School. And I eventually became a professor of English who embraces a Reformed theology, a Wesleyan sensibility, and an Anglican liturgy.

During my first year at Westmont I took a required January-term course called "Christian Perspectives on Learning" (CPOL), in which I took my first tentative steps toward forming my educational philosophy.[13] Initially, I saw Westmont as the ideal *via media* between two Chicago-school theories—John Dewey's pragmatism and Robert Maynard Hutchins's idealism. Dewey's call to learn through experience could be met, I thought, through a journalism internship, working on the *Horizon*, and other extracurricular activities. But I also shared Hutchins's belief that immersion in and conversations about the texts of the great tradition gave me the opportunity to define and examine my experiences, to grow as a complex human being, to be cognizant of culture and history, and to exercise wisdom as I tried to contribute to a better world. Whether I became a journalist or an attorney, and perhaps eventually a politician like my mother, a strong liberal arts education combined with practical experience would provide excellent preparation. In CPOL I also first read a text that I repeatedly returned to in later years: Wheaton College professor Arthur Holmes's *The Idea of a Christian College* (1975). While Hutchins advocated a study of the liberal arts as a way to become fully human, Holmes wrote, "Christian liberal arts education is an invitation to become increasingly a Christian person."[14] I believed that my Westmont education—not in an ivory tower, but in a tropical paradise—was preparing me to serve others eventually. Academic life was a distinctive period of separation from the world in order to prepare to enter the world. This simplistic view of Christian higher education became more complicated over subsequent years.

By the time I graduated from Westmont in 1978, I had worked out a position on the relationship of Christianity and culture with reference to three thinkers: Francis Schaeffer, Jacques Ellul, and Richard

13. Westmont based this course on a similar course at Calvin College, although I did not know this at the time.

14. Arthur F. Holmes, *The Idea of a Christian College*, rev. ed. (Grand Rapids: Eerdmans, 1987), 96–97.

Mouw. Schaeffer had spoken at Westmont in 1965, and the legend of his lederhosen and long hair lived on, along with admiration for his engagement with film and art and his call to exercise a Christian worldview. Numerous Westmont students had made the pilgrimage to L'Abri, and Schaeffer's books were read in several courses. Barry Hankins notes the influential role of Schaeffer on Christian college campuses in the 1970s: "He was one of those responsible for helping evangelicals reject fundamentalist anti-intellectualism in favor of a renewed emphasis on things of the mind and a reengagement with mainstream intellectual culture."[15] I found *The God Who Is There* (1968) a powerful apologetic, but was disappointed with *How Should We Then Live? The Rise and Decline of Western Culture* (1976). In this popular book and accompanying one-million-dollar film series, Schaeffer theorized that as human beings turned away from Christian truth, they collapsed both artistically and scientifically. When people rejected the truth of God, they lost access to any truth, for without God, humanity was incapable of perceiving truth or producing work containing truth.

Schaeffer engaged culture because he talked about Ingmar Bergman and Woody Allen and John Cage, but he had nothing good to say about them, analyzing rather than appreciating, critiquing rather than dialoguing. The specific details of his discussions were frequently inaccurate, which detracted from his argument, but a more serious problem lay in his presuppositions about and attitudes toward culture. Schaeffer justified his approach on the sole, slightly out-of-context verse, "As [a man] thinketh . . . , so is he" (Prov. 23:7 KJV). From this starting point, Schaeffer posited a line of progression: culture originates with philosophy, which then successively infiltrates art, music, general culture, and, finally, theology. Few cultural historians would recognize such a precise evolution. Furthermore, by focusing on the philosophy behind culture, Schaeffer failed to examine other informing components, such as the material world, historical events, or emotional and spiritual experiences. His position could be simply summarized: culture always reflects an underlying philosophical belief.

15. Barry Hankins, *Francis Schaeffer and the Shaping of Evangelical America* (Grand Rapids: Eerdmans, 2008), 234–35.

Consequently, Christians should reject any culture that is based on humanism and instead strive to make "the Christian consensus" the ruling force, the new philosophical base for culture.

The countercultural elements of this argument were appealing, but I thought that it too quickly turned into an outright war against culture. Schaeffer wanted me to look at the iridescent beauty of a Monet and immediately reject its value because Impressionism had a flawed worldview. He wanted me to deny the pure strength and evocative power of Beethoven's music and the haunting sensuality and emotional yearning of Debussy and Chopin. But I could see elements of worth, of truth, of beauty, and of rightness in these works. I didn't have the theological language at this point to talk about common grace or sacramentalism, but I did have a basic compass formed by my family and Reformed upbringing whose arrow was pointing in a different direction from Schaeffer's.

Schaeffer's call for Christians to reject secular culture and form their own culture partially resembled what Jacques Ellul, another influential figure on Christian college campuses in the 1970s, advocated in *The Presence of the Kingdom* (1948). Ellul called for Christians to maintain their unique identity in a community informed by the preaching of the Word and the practice of prayer, a community that stood apart from culture with its concern for means and not ends and its manipulative techniques. However, Ellul did advocate for some forms of interaction with the world. The presence of the kingdom should be manifested by the action of God's people as "salt of the earth," "lights of the world," and "sheep in the midst of wolves." The Christian must work to "preserve" the world (in salt terms): "He [or she] must plunge into social and political problems in order to have an influence on the world, not in the hope of making it a paradise, but simply to make it tolerable."[16] Although Ellul insisted that Christians be involved in culture and society, he remained pessimistic about the outcomes of such action; Christians should not attempt to "bring in" the kingdom of God but merely to make the world orderly enough so that the gospel can be proclaimed. Ellul himself was politically

16. Jacques Ellul, *The Presence of the Kingdom*, trans. Olive Wyon (New York: Seabury, 1967), 47.

active, serving in the French Resistance and later as deputy mayor of Bordeaux. But his call for action was limited. In a sudden shift characteristic of his dialectical method, Ellul wrote, "What matters is to *live* and not to act."[17] The emphasis once again reverted to the spiritual community, the distinctive life of the Christian immersed in Word and prayer. Ellul warned that in revolutionary Christianity, we must not become absorbed in advocating for a cause that would simply replace the status quo. Instead, we should develop a sharp awareness of the world, create a new language for convincing communication, and spread the Christian message through mission activities.

Ellul's concerns for Christians to be grounded in the Word and prayer, to be uniquely set off from society by a way of life, and to live together in self-giving community were valuable, I thought, but Ellul wanted Christian cultural involvement to be limited—to "live and not to act." Ellul, like Schaeffer, seemed to perceive only the corruption in culture and spent much of the book warning about dehumanizing technological advances without acknowledging that technology can be beneficially harnessed. Ellul's call for Christians to interact with society and culture was welcome, but he, like Schaeffer, only warned me of the evils I would find without mentioning the blessings.

The ideas of Richard J. Mouw provided me with a framework for a broader scope of cultural involvement than that offered by either Schaeffer or Ellul. Mouw was not yet the distinguished scholar, educational leader, or evangelical household name he was later to become; he was merely a professor from Calvin College who had written two books on politics. In a series of lectures that he gave at Westmont in 1978 and his book *Politics and the Biblical Drama*, Mouw helped me grasp and then articulate my discomfort with Schaeffer and Ellul. Mouw pointed out that most American evangelicals were culturally alienated, seeing little connection between culture and faith. While Schaeffer and Ellul advocated a continued separation with an alternative or evangelizing response, Mouw proposed a radically different route.

Christians were called to dual citizenship; on one hand we were to be a holy nation and "listen to God's Word, experience the healing provided by the servant-Lord, and grow in grace and knowledge," but

17. Ibid., 92.

we were also citizens of this world and must be "an active presence in the larger community, proclaiming the word [we have] received, responding to the actual needs and suffering [we] find." Being such an "active presence" in the world includes interacting with culture. "A conscious attempt to transform culture lies at the heart of the Christian calling," Mouw wrote. Christians must "paint pictures to the glory of God and write poetry to the glory of God."[18] Mouw reminded me that humanity is "fallen, but created," and the "glory and the honor of the nations" will be brought into the new Jerusalem—culture will be redeemed when Christ returns. Consequently the church should attempt to engage in "empathetic listening" to culture, interpreting and explaining both Word and culture.

Similar to Schaeffer and Ellul in advocating for Christians to prac- tice a distinct way of life, Mouw added a responsibility to redeem culture, pointing out that God's image persists in all people and all culture, despite being warped and, at times, almost indistinct. Like Ellul, Mouw encouraged developing an awareness of the world, but this awareness, he continued, calls us not only to evangelism but also to examine Chinese art, African music, and European literature in order to ascertain the truth they contain and hear the questions they raise. These words were my first gentle nudge to the cultural south; previously I had paid attention to the politics of world events, but I had seldom considered the products of world cultures, content to dwell in the great tradition of Western civilization.

During the second semester of my junior year, I experienced a vo- cational crisis. My political science major required an internship, so I was working with a Santa Barbara legal aid society that assisted elderly clients who were being evicted from their rent-controlled apartments so landlords could raise the rent. I interviewed clients, researched local and state law, and wrote depositions. The attorneys with whom I worked were principled and welcoming, the clients were profuse in their gratitude, and my depositions were lauded for their clarity, organization, and grammar. "There's no doubt that you will make an excellent lawyer," my supervisor told me after a week. This was, I

18. Richard Mouw, *Politics and the Biblical Drama* (Grand Rapids: Eerdmans, 1976), 81.

believed, good work—the kind of work that made a tangible difference in people's lives, that served my neighbor—but I was miserable. I
dreaded every minute in the office, for despite the different individual
human beings with whom I dealt, most of my work involved mind-
numbing repetitions of standard questions, information, and case law.

About the same time as despair set in, one of my English professors, a tall, older gentleman named Arthur Lynip, called me into his
office. I had recently given a class presentation on Faulkner's "The
Bear," and I assumed Dr. Lynip wanted to discuss this. But when I
entered his book-lined office and sat in a faded floral armchair, he
asked, "Susan, have you ever considered becoming a college professor?" I was completely taken aback. When I was growing up, people
often assumed that I would become a teacher, as teaching or becoming
a nurse was the fallback position for intelligent Lynden girls before
they got married, but I knew that I was not gifted at working with
children or adolescents, and I resented the implicit sexism behind
that assumption. But a college professor? Westmont only had two
women professors, both of whom were reserved and undemanding,
and neither had inspired me.

Dr. Lynip continued, "I was impressed with how well you explained
the Faulkner story yesterday. It made me think you could be a gifted
teacher." I left his office with a potential new life narrative to consider.
Over the next week, I thought and prayed and consulted. I examined
the lives of my favorite professors, and I liked what I saw: reading,
writing, and talking about texts; discussing significant ideas with colleagues and students; attending plays with students and having them
over for pizza. I began to realize that I could serve God and others as a
college professor just as much as by being a political activist. I quit my
internship, signed up for additional literature classes, began planning
to write a senior honors thesis, and started studying French. I was
going to go to graduate school to earn a PhD in English literature so
that I could become a professor at a Christian college.

❖ 2 ❖

Going Aboard

1978–86

In the midst of long nights in the *Horizon* office and campus political wrangles, I managed to write a ninety-seven-page senior honors project on Flannery O'Connor, the "Christ-haunted" twentieth-century Southern writer. I wanted to continue to delve into O'Connor's writing, so most of the graduate programs to which I applied were in the South and had senior scholars working in Southern literature. Because O'Connor's fiction was so deeply rooted in her sense of place, I thought my work would be enhanced if I were to live in the South, to "live and breathe [it] in like air," as Faulkner describes.[1] I was also ready to stretch my Lynden-bred wings further. Westmont, Santa Barbara, and Southern California had expanded my horizons, but I was eager to experience another part of the country and to make my first foray into secular education.

Although I hoped to become a professor at a small Christian liberal arts college like Westmont, I was also resigned to the fact that my future employment prospects were bleak. The academic job market in the late 1970s was deplorable, with no relief in sight. A study by the Carnegie Commission on Higher Education, *PhD's and the Academic*

---

1. William Faulkner, *Absalom, Absalom!* (New York: Modern Library, 1936), 361.

Labor Market (1976), was predicting that an oversupply of PhD hold-ers would flood and depress the job market in the 1980s. I was well aware of this dismal fact, but I put myself into God's hands, reason-ing that if I were to be so blessed as to be accepted into a graduate program with full funding, I would enjoy spending the next several years of my life as a student, regardless of whether I eventually found a teaching position or not. I could always go to law school later.

At Westmont, I had fallen in love with a good friend and gotten married, later than many of my Lynden peers, but with no inten-tions of giving up my education, and my husband fully supported my academic interests. I was beginning to recognize the depth of my "intellectual appetite," as Paul Griffiths terms the human longing for knowledge. Opting to go to graduate school for the pure pleasure of learning with only a contingent goal of employment might appear frivolous to some, but I viewed this decision as a way in which I could worship God and use my God-given talents.

Griffiths notes that the early church fathers distinguished between two kinds of intellectual appetite: *curiositas* and *studiositas*, curiosity and studiousness. Curiosity seeks knowledge in order to control or triumph over the material, "but the studious do not seek to sequester, own, possess, or dominate what they hope to know; they want, instead, to participate lovingly in it, to respond to it knowingly as gift rather than as potential possession."[2] Responding to knowledge as gift, we profess God as the gracious gift-giver and name our own creatureliness. I went to graduate school to participate lovingly in great works of literature, to celebrate such works as gifts from a loving God, and to grow in wisdom through such encounters. Graduate study for me was not necessarily preparation for the future so much as a faithful activity in the present, valuable in and of itself. My views of education were changing.

Graduate Study of English Literature

Although I was accepted into several programs, Emory University in Atlanta, Georgia, offered me the most financial support—a bountiful

2. Paul J. Griffiths, *Intellectual Appetite: A Theological Grammar* (Washington, DC: Catholic University of America Press, 2009), 21.

package covering my entire graduate education—so it was easy to discern God's hand opening a door and affirming my growing sense of vocation. After my graduation from Westmont in 1978, my husband and I set off on a road trip during which we camped in a thunderstorm at the Grand Canyon, climbed through the Cliff Dwellings in Mesa Verde, viewed the Midwest from the top of the Gateway Arch in Saint Louis, and broke down in the humid hillbilly country of West Virginia. I was finally seeing America. Arriving in Atlanta to mid-September heat and humidity was a shock after the balmy beauty of Santa Barbara, but we found a shabby apartment in married student housing with a huge, rickety, old window-box air conditioner, and I embarked upon graduate study.

My first-year fellowship paid my tuition and included a small monthly stipend, without requiring anything from me but a devotion to learning. Emory allowed doctoral students a year to adjust to graduate work before assigning them tasks first as either a teaching or research assistant, and later as composition instructors. It was a humane system, which allowed me to turn my attention exclusively to academic pursuits, without extracurricular activities or job responsibilities. All my learning life I had gamboled, scattering my energies far and wide, but now I focused on a single target. Graduate school granted me the physical time and mental space to dedicate myself to becoming a literary scholar. I felt as if I were in heaven.

In the late 1970s, the English graduate program at Emory began with historical coverage of British and American literature, followed by study in a specialized field. At the end of the first year, students took a comprehensive exam informally known as "From Beowulf to Thomas Wolfe." English literature was defined exclusively as literature from either Great Britain or the United States and did not include works written in English from any of the Commonwealth countries, such as Canada, Australia, India, or South Africa. (At this time, a handful of American universities offered programs in Commonwealth literature, which was considered a separate field from English literature.) At Emory, first-year course work was designed to fill the gaps from one's undergraduate curriculum. Thus, despite my interest in Southern American literature, I was consigned my first year to work in early British literature, eighteenth-century satire, and the Victorian novel.

Following the comprehensive exam, terminal MA students wrote a thesis, but those who were moving directly into the PhD program (as I was) enrolled in specialized course work. This process was followed by the construction of a reading list for the doctoral qualifying exams— a reading list that launched the graduate student into dissertation research and extensive work on an even narrower topic.

In my first term at Emory, I was introduced to early British literature by John Miles Foley, a young assistant professor who eventually became one of the world's foremost authorities on comparative oral traditions before his premature death in 2012. Professor Foley taught me that the great epics of the Western tradition, such as *Beowulf* and *The Odyssey*, were originally not physical texts but orature, fluid oral performances that incrementally morphed through the recitations of different singers over many years. A work became solidified when it was transcribed, but the written texts we now read still bore marks of their orality, and their aesthetic achievements and thematic significance were enhanced by learning how to read them in that light. Professor Foley was conducting fieldwork in what was then Yugoslavia, locating, recording, and analyzing narratives recounted by elderly Serbian storytellers in primitive villages. These contemporary singers of tales were practicing the same art as Homer, and from their performances, Professor Foley developed theories regarding oral formulaic composition that he applied to interpreting the ancient classics. Professor Foley's work taught me an indispensable lesson about oral literature that would later help me to understand and appreciate fundamental aspects of African literature.

Emory's Southern literature specialist was a crotchety curmudgeon named Floyd C. Watkins, who had a formidable reputation as one of the most difficult professors at Emory, both academically and personally. An expert in William Faulkner and Robert Penn Warren, Professor Watkins addressed all his students as "Mr." or "Miss" in a low growl and was known for his merciless seminar interrogations, exacting evaluations of written prose, and blunt assessments of the limits of the graduate student mind. Page limits were sacrosanct; if a ten-page paper was assigned, but a student produced eleven pages, Professor Watkins would throw away the final page and grade the essay down because it did not have a conclusion. A faithful Presbyterian, he had high standards for decorum, but he also enjoyed his Jim Beam.

Many students avoided Professor Watkins, but those who did take his seminars and managed to survive his rigor and sarcasm learned from a master. A select few were invited each spring to visit his country log cabin where Professor Watkins relived his youth by chopping wood while wearing faded blue jeans and worn red suspenders. He was a Georgia country boy who had succeeded through education, and he never let anyone forget either of those facts, imperiously playing the part of a plain-spoken, hill-country sage. Professor Watkins took students on Southern literature pilgrimages—to Rowan Oak, Faulkner's home in Oxford, Mississippi; to Georgia's Springer Mountain, the eponymous setting of a deer-hunting poem by James Dickey (author of *Deliverance*, also set in the Georgia hill country); and to Andalusia, the Georgia family farm of Flannery O'Connor.

When we visited in 1979, Andalusia was abandoned and decrepit, but Professor Watkins arranged to have the barbed-wire-topped entrance gate unlocked, and we wandered through peaceful hayfields and past a collapsing peacock aviary, where I found an opulent blue and green peacock feather. O'Connor had been fascinated with peacocks, having as many as fifty peafowl at Andalusia at one time; I like to think that my feather, which I still have today, fell from the tail of a descendent of one of O'Connor's own birds.[3]

In my second year at Emory, I took two seminars from Professor Watkins, one on Southern literature and another on William Faulkner. Floyd liked me: I was punctiliously prepared; wrote clear, organized prose; treated him respectfully; and was a married Christian woman, with a more sedate life than many of my partying peers. Unfortunately, one of the first things I learned about him in Southern Literature was that he detested Flannery O'Connor. She had done a reading at Emory in the 1950s and, as best as we graduate students could determine from Professor Watkins's grumblings, had either been rude to or insulted him. While he taught her short stories in his seminar and included Andalusia in his tours, he didn't have much use for her

---

3. Andalusia has since been restored and is now open to the public. O'Connor's flock died out, and a new peacock aviary was built in 2009. See http://andalusiafarm .org/home.htm.

as an author. He thought she was a bitter old maid who gave the rural South he revered a bad name, and he deemed her characters to be gratuitously grotesque caricatures of good country people. It was soon clear that although Professor Watkins would be happy to work with me, he would not be happy to have me work with Flannery O'Connor. Instead, I would need to do my dissertation on Faulkner.

I was also taking a course during my second year on nineteenth-century American literature with Professor William B. Dillingham, who specialized in the work of Herman Melville. Professor Dillingham was the coauthor, along with Professor Watkins, of the *Practical English Handbook*, one of the standard texts for freshman composition courses across the nation, and the two of them were the department's odd couple, with Professor Dillingham playing Felix to Professor Watkins's Oscar. Professor Dillingham was tall, distinguished, and elegantly at-tired, with a honeyed Southern accent, while Professor Watkins was short, stout, and rumpled, with a Georgia country twang. Professor Dillingham was a perfect gentleman who, as the chair of the English de-partment, calmly smoothed ruffled academic egos. His seminar probed the beauty and truth found in Hawthorne, Dickinson, and Melville, and he gave kindly, judicious advice that gently pushed me toward excellent work. Professor Watkins, on the other hand, was a difficult taskmaster, obstructionist, and erratic. After writing a well-received seminar paper on *Moby-Dick*, I realized that I would experience less drama were I to work with Professor Dillingham and that I would be able to complete my dissertation more quickly with his assistance. While many of my peers were happy to draw out their graduate school experience, I was intent on finishing expeditiously, since going to graduate school was a blessed luxury and my husband was eager to move on with his life. So I became a Melville scholar, working with Professor Dillingham, and completed my PhD in a record four years.

The Rise of Literary Theory

The years I spent in graduate school (1978–82) were a watershed in the study of literature with the occurrence of "the rise of theory." These rapidly shifting intellectual currents were in due time to help me navigate my turn south to the study of African literature. Historically, in American literary studies the center of gravity has shifted from *scholarship* to *criticism* to *theory*. Synchronically, all three activities are complexly related, but chronologically, different elements dominate.

Literary scholarship, in this account, is the uncovering or discovery of new information: a previously unknown letter by Emily Dickinson, an article on the national rhetoric of bridges in the *Atlantic Monthly* that Dickinson might have read, or the doctrinal disputes in the Amherst Congregationalist church in 1860. Such information—biographical details, literary and personal influences, publication and reception history, historical and philosophical contexts, and so on—can illuminate the meaning of texts. *Literary criticism* refers to the study, interpretation, and evaluation of specific works. The critic analyzes and explains the work's meaning and, frequently, judges its worth, value, or achievements. *Criticism* often draws on *scholarship* in order to make or support its interpretive claims; for example, the *Atlantic Monthly*'s essay on bridges might help us develop a new reading of Dickinson's bridge poems. But *literary criticism* also relies upon *literary theory*, a philosophical discussion of the nature, functions, methods, and goals of literature. Assumptions concerning the personal and social value of literature and theories about the relationship of a text to the author, the reader, and the world always lie behind any kind of critical judgment.

The formal study of literature in America began at the end of the nineteenth century, arising from earlier philological and rhetorical studies of classical literature. College students then had parsed Greek to read Homer and studied Cicero to hone their rhetorical skills, but English-language authors such as Chaucer, Shakespeare, and Milton were not part of the curriculum; discussion of their works occurred only in student clubs or literary journals. When English literature, including works by American authors, first became the object of academic study at the birth of the twentieth century, the discipline was divided between the generalists and the philologists—those who studied literature as a way to discuss profound human issues versus those who conducted specialized research.[4] Early graduate training in

4. Gerald Graff, *Professing Literature: An Institutional History* (Chicago: University of Chicago Press, 1987), 55.

English, in an attempt to be as scientific as other emerging disciplines in an era that saw the creation of the college major and increasing academic specialization,[5] emphasized research on textual variants, philological issues, and philosophical, historical, or biographical contexts. *Literary scholarship* was the reigning paradigm.

By the 1930s, however, a group of scholars became impatient with both the humanistic and the historical study of literature because neither provided a strong defense for literature in an age that increasingly privileged science as the way to truth. In an attempt to affirm literature's exclusive power, the movement dubbed "the New Criticism" distinguished literary language from scientific language, the literary object (famously described by Cleanth Brooks as "the well wrought urn") from real life: "[Literature] assumes a necessary place in the life of the civilized man [or woman] because it contains a unique kind of knowledge: he can learn from it that which he can get nowhere else."[6] This is a theoretical claim, although no one was talking about literary theory yet. New Criticism held that the unique knowledge offered by a literary text can be tapped only through detailed analysis of elements such as structure, meter, rhyme, diction, metaphors, ironies, and paradoxes. One need not conduct scholarship into matters outside of the text in order to determine its meaning and value.

New Criticism turned the study of literature away from linguistic, historical, and biographical scholarship to focus on textual interpretation, or criticism. The New Criticism simultaneously offered a rigorous analytical approach suitable for scholars and a practical reading strategy suitable for undergraduates. Cleanth Brooks and Robert Penn Warren's influential textbook *Understanding Poetry* (1938) transformed the teaching of literature in American colleges and universities. As a reading strategy, New Criticism gave undergraduates a way to study and appreciate Keats without knowing anything about either Romanticism or Keats. New Criticism also instigated changes in the literary canon. By examining and celebrating elements of poetry that had previously

5. On this history, see Jon H. Roberts and James Turner, *The Sacred and the Secular University* (Princeton: Princeton University Press, 2000).
6. Thomas Daniel Young, "A Little Divergence: The Critical Theories of John Crowe Ransom and Cleanth Brooks," in *The Possibilities of Order: Cleanth Brooks and His Work*, ed. Lewis Simpson (Baton Rouge: Louisiana State University Press, 1976), 76.

been overlooked or disparaged, such as paradox and irony, the New Critics brought seventeenth-century metaphysical poets such as Donne and Herbert out of canonical obscurity into fresh prominence and paid less attention to eighteenth-century occasional poets such as Pope and Dryden, whose canonical stock fell. New Criticism also supplied fruitful interpretive strategies suited to the complexities of the emerging modern poetry of Eliot, Pound, and Auden.

By the 1960s, a détente had been reached between the New Criticism and literary scholarship, with both practices informing undergraduate education. Biographical background, social contexts, and intellectual history were considered preliminary information that framed a text, which nonetheless could also be studied in purely formal terms. In a course like Introduction to Literature, students might learn how to read the genres of poetry, fiction, and drama apart from any historical context, while other courses, such as American Literary Realism or British Romanticism, took both form and history into account. As Gerald Graff summarizes, "Criticism and history, it was agreed, were complementary, and no sound literary education could forgo either."[7]

However, in advanced literary studies, critical approaches with distinctive underlying theories were vying for position. Frederick Crews's *The Pooh Perplex: A Student Casebook* (1963) provides a tongue-in-cheek depiction of these critical schools in a collection of essays on A. A. Milne's ursine protagonist penned by a fictitious set of ridiculously named English professors (e.g., Duns C. Penwiper). Besides historical, biographical, and source studies, *The Pooh Perplex* contains analyses ranging from Freudian (Christopher Robin's Oedipal complex) to Marxist (Rabbit as capitalist manager) to Aristotelian (the novel has a beginning, middle, and end!). *The Pooh Perplex* also includes an essay called "Oh *Felix Culpa*! The Sacramental Meaning of *Winnie-the-Pooh*," for religious-literary criticism was a common approach in the 1960s.

As an undergraduate, I had learned to enhance my instinctive love of literature with formal reading skills and a sense of literary history. But in my Westmont classes, we didn't talk about other ways to interpret texts or about competing theories of the ontology and

---

7. Graff, *Professing Literature*, 183.

function of literature. Westmont, like most undergraduate institutions at this time, did not offer a course in literary criticism, but when I decided to go to graduate school, I realized that I needed to think more carefully about how I would go about reading, analyzing, interpreting, and critiquing literature. Consequently, during my senior year, I pursued an independent study in literary criticism, focusing on religious-literary criticism.

While literary scholarship had long considered the impact of the Bible or theological debates on specific texts, the field of religious-literary criticism arose with the work of University of Chicago professor Nathan Scott, who compiled earlier essays by several scholars into a series of landmark volumes, beginning with *The New Orpheus: Essays toward a Christian Poetic* (1964). Scott defined the field as asking theoretical questions about the relationships between the literary and the religious aspects of literature and producing interpretations drawing on both literary and religious concepts. By the mid-1970s, a handful of universities—including Chicago, Virginia, and Emory—offered doctoral programs in the field. Religious-literary criticism was produced by mainline and Catholic scholars, but evangelicals had published little on the topic by 1978.[8] As a college senior, I had read no Reformed scholars on the relationship of literature, criticism, and faith.

Religious-literary criticism as it was first articulated fell into two camps. Some critics, such as Scott, held that the task of the literary critic was to identify the underlying theology inherently contained in all great literary works. Authors' beliefs, their Tillichean "ultimate concerns," determined what they wrote. The New Critics (and Marxist and Freudian critics, for that matter) "forget that writers use language with reference to what they know and feel and believe and . . . we can therefore understand their poems and novels only if we have some appreciation of how their beliefs have operated in enriching the meaning of the words they employ."[9] Such approaches were not revolutionary when it came to Christian poets such as Donne, Milton, and Herbert, but the religious-literary critics were at their

8. Leland Ryken's first book on the relationship of Christianity and literature, *Triumphs of the Imagination: Literature in Christian Perspective*, was published in 1978.

9. Nathan Scott, ed., *The New Orpheus: Essays toward a Christian Poetic* (New York: Sheed & Ward, 1964), 160.

most innovative in interpretations of the alienation, suffering, and despair of twentieth-century literature as cryptically religious. Drawing on biographical background and authorial intention, such critics often spent more time theologizing than reading literary texts in their aesthetic and historical complexity and had a distressing tendency to turn every image into a religious symbol and every suffering man into a Christ figure.

The second camp of religious-literary critics agreed with New Criticism's distinction between art and life, shared its focus on the text, and was equally reluctant to draw conclusions from biographical information. Like the New Critics, they argued that literature contains a special essence that can only be detected through formal analysis. Then, as T. S. Eliot writes in "Religion and Literature," textual interpretation should be "completed" by criticism from an ethical and theological standpoint. "Literary" and "ethical" criticism are two distinct, but complementary, methods of analysis, both of which Christian readers should employ: "What I believe to be incumbent upon all Christians is the duty of maintaining consciously certain standards and criteria of criticism over and above those applied by the rest of the world; and that by these criteria and standards everything that we read must be tested."[10] The moralistic approach could easily disintegrate into a Schaefferean condemnation of the writer's worldview or the content of the work. And when readers judged literature by its degree of Christianity, distortions became frequent.

The best religious-literary critics from this period examine the text's formal elements; weigh biographical, historical, and cultural contexts; and are reluctant to moralize too quickly. For C. S. Lewis, both form and content are crucial; literary works are "not merely *logos* (something said) but *poiema* (something made). . . . To value them chiefly for reflections which they may suggest to us or morals we may draw from them, is a flagrant instance of 'using' instead of 'receiving.' . . . One of the prime achievements in every good fiction has nothing to do with truth or philosophy."[11] Lewis advises critics to enter into the total "primary literary experience" of the work with neutrality: "We

10. T. S. Eliot, "Religion and Literature," in ibid., 233–34.
11. C. S. Lewis, *An Experiment in Criticism* (Cambridge: Cambridge University Press, 1961), 82–83.

must empty our minds and lay ourselves open."[12] Lewis's concern, as contrasted with Eliot's, lies not in a moral evaluation following the literary assessment, but in having the reader partake of the opinions, attitudes, and emotions of the author. A literary text functions as a window allowing us to look at the world through another's eyes, even if we disagree with that person's perspective. Lewis thinks that many texts contain "sub-Christian"—that is, almost Christian—truths, but he also sees value in the vicarious experience of different viewpoints.

When I entered Emory in 1978, faint traces of theory were in the air, but the total transformation of graduate studies had not yet occurred. As Vincent Leitch explains,

> a wave of Continental ideas started sweeping American criticism during the 1960s, cresting throughout the 1970s and 1980s as hermeneutics, semiotics, deconstruction, Neo-Marxism, Lacanian psychoanalysis, German reception theory, and French feminism gained growing numbers of adherents. . . . [F]rom the late 1960s to the early 1980s, the growing importance and centrality within academic literary studies of theory resulted in its constituting the acknowledged vanguard, if not the core, of the discipline.[13]

With so many different questions, practices, and resulting schools, the quintessence of literary theory is difficult to convey, but three points are worth noting. First, literary theory prompted critics to be more aware of the presuppositions they brought to their reading and study of literature. Different assumptions about forms and genres, the role of the reader, and the impact of context (historical, economic, material, psychological, religious, political, etc.) led to different kinds of reading.

Second, new understandings of language as a constructed, not a natural, sign led to more sophisticated versions of New Criticism's textual preoccupation, from semiotics to structuralism to post-structuralism to deconstruction. The key difference came in the fact that newer theories applied to all written texts, drawing no distinctions between literary and scientific language.

12. Ibid., 116.
13. Vincent Leitch, *American Literary Criticism since the 1930s*, 2nd ed. (New York: Taylor & Francis, 2009), 326–27.

Third, theory demonstrated the myriad ways in which forces outside an individual author's conscious intentions entered into the making of meaning, both in the creation and the reception of the text. For religious-literary criticism, theory offered new ways to think about religious belief, theological traditions, and literary production; phenomenology and hermeneutics gave rise to innovative religious ways of reading; and postmodern and deconstructive theories prompted an equation of the inherent undecidability of texts with spiritual mystery and apophatic theology. The rise of theory so complicated and fragmented the study of religion and literature that it is impossible to define it as a coherent field of study today.[14]

Emory's program offered only one optional seminar in literary theory, which I took, studying structuralism; hermeneutics; deconstruction; and Marxist, Freudian, and feminist theory. While Emory graduate students were primarily trained to do close textual, historical, and biographical scholarship, a few newer approaches were gaining traction. Among the faculty, there were tensions between old-guard historical scholars and avant-garde structuralists. Several graduate students were ardent neo-Marxists of the Raymond Williams school, and I was surprised to discover how much I had in common with them in our shared beliefs that literature had moral, social, and political consequences beyond its aesthetic achievements and that the economically privileged should show compassion to others. When my husband lost his job and we were perilously close to subsistence rations, the Marxists kept us fed and in good spirits, despite our frequent arguments about the existence of God. Emory also had its share of feminists and a handful of graduate students pursuing African American studies. Guest lecturers ran the gamut of critical positions—from the legendary anthologist and Romantic scholar M. H. Abrams to one of the rising stars of the Yale School of deconstruction, J. Hillis Miller.

The Religion and Literature program at Emory was housed in the interdisciplinary Graduate Institute of the Liberal Arts (ILA). I had

14. The diverging directions in discussions of religion/theology/Christianity and/ in literature are evident in a special issue of *Religion and Literature* addressing "what sorts of intellectual projects, disciplinary configurations, and scholarly practices might be called into being by thinking about religion and literature together" (Susannah Brietz Monta, "Introduction," *Religion and Literature* 41, no. 2 [2009]: 1).

chosen to apply to the English program rather than to the ILA because I thought a traditional disciplinary focus and opportunities to teach would better prepare me for a college teaching career. But I did hope to take a few ILA courses. Again, I was disappointed. Emory's English department looked down on the ILA, considering their courses less rigorous, and there was only one professor working in Religion and Literature, Robert Detweiler, who was frequently off campus with visiting engagements. So I did no course work in religion and literature.

However, when I began to work on my dissertation, my interest was hooked by Melville's notorious "quarrel with God"[15] and the scripturally infused prose of *Moby-Dick*. One of the prevalent issues in Melville studies at that time was the narration of *Moby-Dick*. As a first-person narrator, Ishmael is quirky; he disappears from the dramatic action midway through the book, he reports scenes and conversations that he could not have witnessed, and his prose style varies erratically. Nineteenth-century reviewers attributed this narrational mayhem to Melville's lack of artistic skill. Twentieth-century critics, more open to paradox and ambiguity, thought Melville was purposefully experimenting with structure and form, was casting Ishmael as a linguistic trickster, or was depicting a Kantian Ishmael, who changed reality as he perceived it.[16]

Professor Dillingham had written of both Ishmael and Coleridge's Ancient Mariner as crazed raconteurs compelled to tell their stories over and over.[17] As graduate students often do, I built my approach on my mentor's, arguing that Ishmael was a prophetic narrator. His frenzied tone, occasionally omniscient viewpoint, and oddities of narration were prophetic traits, not artistic lapses on Melville's part. To support this claim, I researched biographical, literary, social, and historical ideas about prophecy, examining Melville's reading ma-

15. Lawrance Thompson, *Melville's Quarrel with God* (Princeton: Princeton University Press, 1952).

16. Richard H. Brodhead, *Hawthorne, Melville, and the Novel* (Chicago: University of Chicago Press, 1976); Warwick Wadlington, *The Confidence Game in American Literature* (Princeton: Princeton University Press, 1975); and Paul Brodtkorb Jr., *Ishmael's White Whale: A Phenomenological Reading of Moby-Dick* (New Haven: Yale University Press, 1965).

17. William B. Dillingham, "The Narrator of *Moby-Dick*," *English Studies* 49 (1968): 28.

terial, contemporary prophets such as the Millerites and the Shakers, and biblical prophets and prophecy. With extensive archival work, I located an original source text—a popular nineteenth-century dream book consulted by sailors as a key to interpreting their dreams. My dissertation culminated with an interpretation of *Moby-Dick* as prophetically proclaiming that in an inherently ambiguous world, single-minded truth too quickly turned into a destructive monomania. The questions I asked about *Moby-Dick* could have been asked by anyone, but my faith and familiarity with the Christian tradition led me to probe these issues.

Teaching in the Castle in the Clouds

When I went on the job market in 1982, despite having a couple of interviews from both public and private institutions, I received only one offer of employment: as an assistant professor at Covenant College, perched on picturesque Lookout Mountain above Chattanooga, Tennessee, in a former resort hotel called "Castle in the Clouds." Covenant was a small Christian liberal arts college affiliated with the Presbyterian Church of America, which didn't impress my graduate mentors, who tried to convince me to take a one-year position as an instructor at Emory so that I could go on the job market again the following year. But since I had identified a vocation as a Christian college professor, I was thrilled to get the Covenant position. The college had an enrollment of about five hundred students, and I would be half of a two-member English department, teaching four courses a semester. During my interview weekend I met the woman I was replacing, who darkly hinted about the difficulties of being a female professor at Covenant. I had no idea what she was talking about.

The four years I spent at Covenant (1982–86) transformed my intellectual and professional life in three ways: (1) I became a Christian feminist, (2) I discovered African literature, and (3) I realized that my vocation involved scholarship as well as teaching.

Before I began teaching, I had not embraced the feminism of the 1970s, although I was aware of the passionate national debates, particularly over the Equal Rights Amendment, and had several ardent feminist friends. My attitude was both naive and self-absorbed: I had never personally experienced discrimination and was just as capable as any man; if women writers were any good, their works would have made it into the literary canon; the words *man* or *he* could be gender-neutral; the Bible clearly prohibited women from preaching and instructed wives to submit to their husbands. I thought that women might occasionally be treated unfairly, but all in all, twentieth-century American women had a good life.

At Covenant, I was the only woman professor on a faculty of about forty. That didn't bother me initially, but I was slightly irritated when my first committee assignment was to the Social Committee, responsible for planning the Christmas party and end-of-the-year celebration. Social planning was not my forte; I was much more interested in issues addressed by the Curriculum or Admissions Committees. And although Covenant (and Southern) etiquette called for professors to be addressed as "Dr.," students, faculty, and staff continually referred to me as "Mrs. Gallagher." I was slightly shocked after my first two weeks when a belligerent male student told me, on allegedly Christian grounds, that I didn't have the right to teach him, since I was a woman. I suggested that the administration apparently felt otherwise and that he drop my class.

But I didn't have time to worry about feminism, for my first two years at Covenant were a nonstop scramble to prepare for a constantly changing lineup of courses, many of which were completely out of my area of expertise: I taught Journalism, Twentieth-Century Literature, the Victorian Era, Shakespeare, the English Novel, and Introduction to British Literature, in addition to Composition, American Literature, and a Special Topics course in Melville. I soon developed the mantra that years later I was to repeat *ad nauseam* at new-faculty development workshops: "Even if you've never even read the text before, you know more than they do."

The whip-smart, academically hungry, socially confused women students at Covenant were ultimately what made me a feminist. My first step was to put more thought into choosing the texts I would teach to these young women, rather than merely assigning the authors that I had been taught in the male-dominated canon. In doing so, I was following a path I established my first year at Covenant when I resolved to move beyond my graduate training in American literature, which began with Emerson and Thoreau, to assign earlier Christian writers such as Bradford, Bradstreet, Rowlandson, Taylor, and Wheatley because they addressed issues of faith, doubt, suffering, providence, and endurance. I did not jettison the American transcendentalists or naturalists, but spent less time on them in order to incorporate more clearly Christian voices into the course readings. Reading, I had come to believe, involved more than escape and delight; it could help a reader become the self that God had created her or him to be.

Similarly, when I taught the Special Topics course my second year, I designed a new course, Fiction by Women, rather than repeating my Melville course, even though I had to patch together a variety of texts, as no standard anthology was available. In giving priority to Christian writers or women writers, I was practicing what some derided as "identity politics," choosing texts to teach because of the author's social, cultural, or religious location. Literary traditionalists argued that course texts should be selected purely on aesthetic, not political grounds. However, graduate school had taught me that there were many ways in which aesthetic achievement could be defined, and I also believed that the expression of ideas in texts was equally important. Beauty did not trump truth.

My reason for offering Fiction by Women was simple: most of my students were women, and I wanted them to have the opportunity to read women writers and ponder issues related to their own lives. Granted, I also wanted my students to learn about people other than themselves; in fact, I thought that my lily-white classes needed to read African American literature, should consider Elizabethan ideas, and could learn much from *Moby-Dick*. But the traditional literary canon regnant in the 1980s asked for more empathetic stretching from women than from men. It required women to spend more time looking out of other people's windows than into mirrors illuminating their own experiences. I began to incorporate more women's texts in my American literature survey, even though the only American women writers I had studied in graduate school were Flannery O'Connor, Eudora Welty, and Emily Dickinson.

Facing my students, I began to wonder, why *were* there so few women in the traditional canon? The publication in 1985 of *The*

Norton Anthology of Women Writers, along with the critical and historical perspectives in *The New Feminist Criticism*, introduced me to one version of the feminist literary tradition and gave me interpretive strategies and aesthetic measures for women's texts. As Nina Baym asserted, "Assessments of American literature have been biased in favor of things male—in favor, say, of whaling ships rather than the sewing circle as a symbol of human community . . . displaying an exquisite compassion for the crisis of the adolescent male, but altogether impatient with the parallel crises of the female."[18] Perhaps ambiguity, complexity, and paradox were not always the highest artistic qualities; perhaps simplicity, domestic images, and lucid emotional representations had value as well. I was nonetheless struck by the incongruity that many of the new feminists blamed Christianity for women's oppression, terming it a patriarchal system, but failed to see that the nineteenth-century women writers they were recovering and praising often drew on Christian commitments, imagery, and language to justify uplifting the downtrodden, opposing oppression, and expressing themselves.

Once I started reading feminist criticism, the issue of sexist language, as it was then called, wasn't far behind. (Today the term *gender-inclusive language* is preferred.) I read extensively in the debates, and although I didn't think *genkind* had much of a future, Casey Miller and Kate Swift's *Handbook of Nonsexist Writing* (1980) soon became my guide.[19] For me, the most convincing argument for adopting nonsexist language came from studies that showed children's and adolescents' confusion over the gender-inclusive use of *man* and *he*. Before a certain age, children were unable to distinguish the difference between the male *he* and the inclusive *he*, which meant they often assumed and were socialized to believe that boys could do things that girls could not. This was especially brought home to me when an older male student who had been resisting my efforts to teach gender-inclusive writing told me that his six-year-old daughter had come to him in tears, wanting to know why Jesus loved boys more than girls. "The

18. Nina Baym, *Woman's Fiction: A Guide to Novels by and about Women in America, 1820–70*, 2nd ed. (Urbana: University of Illinois Press, 1993), xiii–xiv.
19. Casey Miller and Kate Smith had prompted a national debate with their *New York Times* essay, "Is Language Sexist? One Small Step for Genkind," April 16, 1972.

Sunday school teacher said that Jesus died to save all mankind," she wept. "What about little girls?"

Although my female students regularly told me that using *man* and *he* to refer to all of God's people didn't bother them, I worried about such language's implicit effects; if women always heard a student referred to as *he*, would they feel less able to accomplish their academic goals? Why were my female students typically so insecure and self-deprecating about their academic abilities? I wanted to convince all my students that both females and males are equal in God's sight and have been given intellectual gifts. I wanted my language to glorify God and express my love for other people, so I learned and taught how to avoid sexist language in speech and writing.

Becoming a Christian Feminist

By my third year at Covenant, I was dealing with a steady stream of female students inundating my office, desperate to talk about ideas, friendship, dating, careers, and faith. One asked me to supervise her senior project on biblical feminism, so I began to study the biblical texts about women and to read books debating these issues, including the groundbreaking *All We're Meant to Be* (1974), by Letha Scanzoni and Nancy Hardesty, and the counterarguments of Susan T. Foh in *Women and the Word of God: A Response to Biblical Feminism* (1979).

The book that had the greatest impact on me, however, was *Women at the Crossroads: A Path beyond Feminism and Traditionalism* (1982), by Kari Torjesen Malcolm. Criticizing both feminism's focus on the autonomous self in search of fulfillment and traditionalism's consignment of a woman's identity to her relationships with men, Malcolm called Christian women to recognize the foundational truths that they were created in the image of God, that in Christ there is no difference between women and men, and that a woman's most important role is to be faithful to the gifts and calling she has received from God. Christian women, Malcolm claimed, too often idolized home and family, finding their identity there, rather than in God, while secular feminists idolized career and self, finding their identity there, rather than in God.

My biblical studies revealed how Jesus countered the subordinate role of women in Jewish society by treating them as equals and that a basic principle found in both the creation account and Galatians 3:28 was that men are not superior to women. When it came to human identity as God's image, the Bible endorsed equality, but when it came to specific roles in marriage or church, the biblical evidence was unclear, confusing, and sometimes contradictory. Issues of translation, social and cultural norms, and universal versus contextual principles muddied the waters.

Although I was not yet sure that women ought to be ordained, I was convinced they could be deacons, and I had no misgivings about my role as a professor at a Christian college. Consequently, when I was asked to speak in chapel in the fall of 1985, I felt no qualms, for chapel was not a church but an educational worship space. I was speaking as part of a series on building relationships, which is probably why I was asked to talk—to give the female perspective—and I had been appalled by an earlier chapel talk referring to college "men" and "girls" and extolling finding a Christian spouse while attending college. I countered that one's main goal as a college student should not be to get married, even if that might be a pleasant side effect. "Your most important goal," I told five hundred captive students, "is to grow intellectually, to become a better Christian thinker." And when it came to building relationships, college offered an exceptional opportunity to develop intellectual friendships. I concluded, "In developing male/female relationships, we need to remember to treat everyone as image bearers of God—complete with intellectual, emotional, and social sides. Try to get to know people as people, not as potential dates." College needed to emphasize the head as well as the heart.

I wasn't prepared for the response my address provoked. Students I didn't know stopped me to tell me how much they liked it; my classes wanted to discuss the issues I raised rather than the course material; the college president called me to talk about relationships on campus; the faculty Social Committee (on which I no longer served) asked me "to share my wisdom" about how to make the campus social atmosphere better. I found such enthusiasm elating at first, but gradually I began to feel a burden of being *the* female authority on relationships, as if I had everything figured out, and I didn't think that I had. That burden grew stronger when I agreed two weeks later to lead a small group chapel on "Being a Woman and a Christian." Students could meet part of Covenant's chapel requirement by participating in one of a series of small groups led by faculty and staff on Thursday mornings. But when I showed up that first morning, more than one hundred women were trying to squeeze into a thirty-person classroom. We moved to a lecture hall, but I was distressed by the desperate need of these women for someone to talk with them about these issues. My "small" group chapel attracted more than one hundred students for the rest of the semester and brought even more students to my congested office hours.

As I talked with these college women, I began to realize that we all often acted as if we weren't the equals of our male peers. We were afraid to be too assertive, afraid that we might be labeled with the Christian college *f*-word (*feminist*). But we were just as valuable and gifted and blessed in God's eyes. I became convinced that even though I might be seen as a radical feminist (which was far from the case), it was my obligation to stand up for God's image in me, whenever possible articulating my reasons for doing so, but without fear of being labeled. So I made a small professional change; I began to insist that people call me "Dr. Gallagher," because my PhD was a God-given gift that should be celebrated. Just because I was a woman didn't make my academic credentials any different from those of my male colleagues, all of whom were addressed as "Dr." whether or not they had earned their doctorate. And, I realized, it was important for my female students to see me affirming my academic standing.

Introduction to South African Literature

Although less dramatic initially, a second shift in my professional identity was set into motion during my fourth year at Covenant when I taught a South African literature course. Curricular demands gave birth to this course, but it inaugurated a major new direction in my scholarly trajectory. Because Covenant had such limited faculty resources, it had an odd curricular component requiring students to take either two semesters of a foreign language—not enough to develop any level of proficiency but enough to expose them to a different culture—or two courses in literature or music from a different culture. Consequently, each English professor needed to offer one course in a literature other than American or British, such as French drama or the Russian novel, taught in translation if necessary. Faced with developing another course from scratch without graduate preparation, I decided to teach South African literature.

My high school and undergraduate political interests had never completely waned, although they had been temporarily eclipsed during the intensity of graduate school. I had closely followed the maelstrom of events in South Africa and the vibrant international anti-apartheid movement. By the mid-1980s, the South African situation was reaching its violent nadir, with protest marches, school boycotts, township riots, guerrilla bombings, and government reprisals. Sixteen months of chaos following the 1976 Soweto uprising had climaxed with Steve Biko's death in detention in 1977. The nonstop picket of the South African embassy in London, national furor over economic sanctions and disinvestment, and the controversial international sports boycott filled the print and broadcast media. Images of relentlessly advancing tanks, of dark smoke from burning tires and bombed shopping centers, and of South African security forces wielding batons, tear gas, and machine guns entered American living rooms each evening. The anti-apartheid movement saturated popular consciousness in the 1980s; Theo Huxtable, the amiable teenage son in the *Cosby Show*, had a "Free Mandela!" poster in his bedroom, and when his fictional sister Sondra had twins, they were named Nelson and Winnie.

My own concern for South Africa had more personal roots. As a third-generation Dutch American raised in a community dominated by the Christian Reformed Church, I felt reverberations of responsibility and guilt about South Africa. My Dutch great-aunt had been one of the European bush pilots who opened up the southern tip of Africa to economic expansion after the Second World War. The CRC had spent thirty years agonizing over its relationship to its sister churches in South Africa before declaring in 1985 that apartheid was a sin and any attempt to justify apartheid theologically was a heresy. Following this declaration, the question of the CRC's fellowship status with South African Reformed churches was a matter of heated debate, not resolved until 1989, and *The Reformed Journal*, which I read loyally, was full of commentary and debates about the South African situation. What, I wondered, could I do, what was I called to do, as a faithful Christian? I had supported Emory's disinvestment campaign, but I wasn't able personally to picket embassies, do humanitarian work in South Africa, or challenge the Afrikaner political system.

My sense of social responsibility was, undoubtedly, part of the popular national fascination with South Africa, and my parents' political activism also played a role. But my primary inspiration came from Nicholas Wolterstorff's *Until Justice and Peace Embrace* (1983), which I read in 1984–85 with a study group of Covenant professors and spouses. This book, my first exposure to Wolterstorff's thought, prompted me to think about my vocation of teaching in fresh ways and provided my first taste of neo-Calvinist thought. Comparing liberation theology and neo-Calvinism as two versions of "world-formative Christianity," Wolterstorff noted that both expressed concern for the victims of modern society, "not by applying bandages, but by searching out what it was that inflicted the wounds and seeking to effect changes in that quarter."[20] This was reminiscent of my Marxist friends at Emory who were as concerned about changing unjust structures as they were about helping people. For too much of the twentieth century, Wolterstorff claimed, American Christianity had taken the bandage approach, and he wanted to reclaim the social vision of the Reformed tradition as articulated by both John Calvin and Abraham Kuyper, the nineteenth-century Dutch theologian, politician, and philosopher.

Wolterstorff's personal comments in his preface resonated with my own experience: "As I was growing up in the Reformed tradition, I saw very little of that world-formative impulse so prominent in its origins. For me the tradition represented a certain theology and a certain piety."[21] At its roots, Wolterstorff argued, Calvinism endorsed a world-formative Christianity that called believers to respond to poverty and reform society according to the Word of God by working to establish a world of peace and justice. That could only be done if we understood what inflicted the wounds by tracing historical movements; theorizing about social, political, and economic structures; and analyzing current realities.

20. Nicholas Wolterstorff, *Until Justice and Peace Embrace* (Grand Rapids: Eerdmans, 1983), 65.
21. Ibid., ix.

Most crucially, we needed to have a clear vision of God's goal for the world: the vision of *shalom*—"the human being dwelling at peace in all his or her relationships: with God, with self, with fellows, with nature."[22] In his discussion of how a Christian should respond to a world characterized by poverty, injustice, and violence, Wolterstorff discussed the South African situation at several points. *Until Justice and Peace Embrace* impelled me to ask how I could work for change, justice, and peace. Was my vocation in teaching students how to read and write, how to appreciate and appropriate literature, an aspect of world-formative Christianity? Wouldn't it be better to be training students to be doctors, social workers, or politicians? Such questions were haunting me when I learned I needed to offer a course in literature other than British or American, and my impatience to do something besides watch and pray found an outlet. Since my talents and training were in analyzing, interpreting, and teaching literature, I decided to employ those strengths to serve in the field in which I found myself planted. I didn't know much about South African literature, other than the work of Alan Paton, but I knew that two South African writers— Nadine Gordimer and J. M. Coetzee—were receiving international critical attention. So I set out to educate myself about South African literature and its role in the current political and social struggle.

Reading South African literature, I soon realized, had the potential to open my students' minds and their hearts, raising their awareness and understanding of a contemporary instance of oppression with significant religious reverberations. While not discounting South African literature's capacity to teach us truths about ourselves, to be a mirror, I thought it could also function as a window, opening our eyes to experiences other than our own. Reading literature also allowed us to hear voices that had been deliberately silenced as a means of denying human identity, to listen to painful but foreign truths. Such reading had the potential to produce both knowledge and empathy, could affect both head and heart. As voters, consumers, church members, and mission supporters, my students were active in world-formation. Novels, stories, plays, and poems portrayed the historical, cultural, and religious roots of the South African situation, educating readers about

22. Ibid., 69–70.

the realities of life under apartheid; tracing the historical struggles among the Afrikaners, British, East Indians, and different indigenous people groups; and elucidating the systems of economic and social control exercised through apartheid legislation. But literature could also convey the paradoxes and pain of a person labeled "coloured" or "Zulu" or "Xhosa" with a richness and nuance unavailable in a sociology or history text, incarnating human reality.

Yet besides giving students a deeper understanding of the origins and aims of apartheid and its opposition, reading South African literature was also a way in which my students could mourn for human sin and suffering. My own initial impulse, I saw, was to take action, to *do something*, and informed action was certainly important, but I also was beginning to understand the value of the sorrow produced through textual encounters. Reading in the Western tradition has been traditionally ruled, as Wolterstorff describes it, by a central motif of liberation—reading liberates us from our parochial particularities into the great cultural heritage of humanity and universal human consciousness. But, as Wolterstorff continues, this practice is deficient in that it does not respond "adequately to the wounds of humanity—in particular the moral wounds; none gives adequate answer to our cries and tears."[23]

One role of the Christian is to share in the sorrow of the oppressed and suffering. In the face of Mary and Martha's bone-piercing grief over the death of their brother, Jesus wept, even though he knew Lazarus would shortly rise from the tomb. Christians are to "mourn with those who mourn" (Rom. 12:15). Literature that articulates the physical, mental, and social conditions of oppression helps us to sorrow. The emotions and situations of fictional characters illuminate the emotions and situations of factual people, help us to glimpse the experience of someone completely different from ourselves.

For my students, reading newspaper accounts about the atrocious conditions in black townships, adding up statistics about the distribution of land and wealth, or even witnessing South African security forces clubbing black protestors on television did not bring home

23. Nicholas Wolterstorff, *Educating for Shalom: Essays on Christian Higher Education* (Grand Rapids: Eerdmans, 2004), 22.

the anguish of South Africans in the same way as did reading Alan Paton's *Cry, the Beloved Country*, Alex La Guma's *A Walk in the Night*, or J. M. Coetzee's *Waiting for the Barbarians*. While reading South African literature was often grim and difficult, and there were many days that we all arrived in class experiencing pain and sorrow, I also witnessed my students developing a genuine awareness and love for their fellow human beings.

By the end of four years at Covenant College, I had recognized one more truth: although I had gone to graduate school hoping to become a teacher at a Christian college to help students grow intellectually, emotionally, and spiritually, I was also called to be a scholar. I had published one peer-reviewed essay on Faulkner in graduate school, but at Covenant I only managed to eke out one piece of scholarship—a short note based on the new source for *Moby-Dick* that I had identified, which was published in *American Literature*. I did a few conference papers on Flannery O'Connor and Melville, kept a notebook jammed with ideas, and began writing an occasional book review for *The Reformed Journal*. But I was itching to write more.

Taking a job at a large public institution with high expectations for research and scholarship, where the publish-or-perish mentality ran deep, where one had to produce at least one if not two books in order to receive tenure, as some of my graduate school friends had done, was not an appealing alternative to a position at an institution like Covenant, but my highly demanding teaching load (in both breadth as well as quantity), the limited support for and encouragement of research and scholarship, and the increasing burden and sense of isolation of being the only female faculty member were stirring a need for change. I loved my students and my colleagues, but I was tired. I began to explore the possibility of faculty positions at larger Christian colleges. The ship I had boarded was leaving the dock.

❖ 3 ❖

The Advocate

1986–93

In June 1983, after my first year at Covenant, I had attended a one-week workshop on "Christianity and Literary Theory," cosponsored by the Coalition for Christian Colleges (which later became the Council for Christian Colleges and Universities [CCCU]) and the National Endowment for the Humanities (NEH). This was part of a series of discipline-based workshops in the humanities funded by the NEH, a program that was to do much to advance the work of Christian scholarship over the next few decades despite the NEH's rejection of several follow-up proposals, perhaps on the grounds that such work turned out to be too sectarian. Twentieth-century Christian scholarship was in its infancy in the 1980s; the Pew Evangelical Scholars Initiative wasn't established until 1991; Mark Noll's *The Scandal of the Evangelical Mind* didn't appear until 1995, with George Marsden's *The Outrageous Idea of Christian Scholarship* published in 1997.

"Christianity and Literary Theory" was led by Arthur Holmes, professor of philosophy at Wheaton College, and James Barcus, professor of English at Baylor University, and the seminar plunged me back into the intoxicating world of graduate school, with the difference that we discussed the increasingly important topic of literary theory explicitly in relationship to Christian faith. During a hot, sticky week at the now-defunct Barrington College in Rhode Island, I met, for the first time, other women who taught at Christian colleges. Betsy Morgan, from Eastern, and Gloria Bell, from Southern Wesleyan, were quick to offer warm friendship, wise counsel, and emotional support.

I also discovered an intellectual affinity with James Vanden Bosch, who was leaving a position at Dordt College to join the Calvin College faculty that fall. We often approached theoretical questions similarly, scrutinizing the presuppositions behind literary theories, affirming the study of literature that challenged or denied Christian ideas, and finding truth, grace, and beauty, with the help of the Holy Spirit, in texts other than the Scriptures. When he learned that I grew up in Lynden, Jim's hearty belly-laugh filled the room. "Why, you're Reformed, Susan," he said. "That explains it." At this moment, Faulkner's words about the South seemed apropos: "*you knew it all already, had learned, absorbed it already without the medium of speech somehow from having been born and living beside it, with it, as children will and do.*"[1] Despite my attempts to leave Lynden behind, I had a Reformed-shaped mind. In graduate school, I had tried to be honest and faithful in my study of literature, but I had never defined my approach specifically as Reformed. But now I began to explore and contemplate what it meant to be a scholar in the Reformed tradition.

Several other people whom I met at Barrington were to play formative roles in my professional life. In later years I had the privilege of working alongside Arthur Holmes at annual CCCU New Faculty Workshops; Jim Barcus invited me to teach a summer graduate seminar on Hawthorne and Melville at Baylor; and Karen Longman and Ken Shipps, from the CCCU staff, were instrumental in my appointment to the planning committee for a new CCCU-sponsored introductory textbook series, *Through the Eyes of Faith*, whose general editor was Nicholas Wolterstorff.

At those planning meetings in Washington, DC, I met Edward Ericson Jr., chair of the English department at Calvin College, who

1. William Faulkner, *Absalom, Absalom!* (New York: Modern Library, 1936), 212–13.

eventually offered me a one-year visiting position in 1986–87. Calvin typically used these visiting positions to audition potential tenure-track faculty members. Although I worried that I might not have the scholarly abilities that Calvin expected, and that Calvin's larger size would not allow the close interactions with students that I had enjoyed at Covenant, my teaching would be limited to my areas of expertise—American literature, the English novel, and composition—and my yearning to write and publish would find fiscal support and collegial encouragement. If I wanted to become a serious teacher-scholar operating from a position of faith, Calvin would provide the best environment in which to do so.

The irony of my working at Calvin College, the last place in the world I had wanted to go when I was a high school senior in Lynden, did not escape me, and I worried about the overwhelming Dutch ethos of both the school and the Grand Rapids community. Did I want to return to a cultural enclave? How would my non-Dutch husband fit in? I could play Dutch bingo—identifying one's Dutch familial and social connections—with the best, but did I want to? How would my emerging Christian feminism play in Grand Rapids? Would Calvin prove to be a stifling environment?

Life and Thought at Calvin College

Despite all of my concerns, I discovered that the Calvin of the 1980s was a markedly different community than the Lynden of the 1960s. In *Dutch Calvinism in Modern America*, James Bratt chronicles a persistent struggle between two factions of Dutch American Calvinists in the twentieth century, the progressives and the traditionalists. Both followed Kuyper in affirming that Christianity was not confined to a religious realm but addressed "every sphere of life"—science, politics, scholarship, and art. All these pursuits were genuine Christian callings, or as Kuyper famously proclaimed, "There is not a square inch in the whole domain of our human existence over which Christ, who is Sovereign over all, does not cry: 'Mine!'"[2] Both parties advocated the cen-

2. Abraham Kuyper, "Sphere Sovereignty," in *Abraham Kuyper: A Centennial Reader*, ed. James D. Bratt (Grand Rapids: Eerdmans, 1998), 488.

trality of a world-and-life view, an operative philosophy that ultimately stemmed from a response to God, and insisted that no intellectual activity was objective, value-free, or without presuppositions.

But the progressives and traditionalists concentrated, respectively, on two central Kuyperian ideas standing in paradoxical tension. The progressives championed the cause of common grace, the belief that in addition to God's special grace bestowed upon the elect for salvation, God also abundantly pours out common grace through all of creation—a grace that sustains the world: "He causes his sun to rise on the evil and the good, and sends rain on the righteous and the unrighteous" (Matt. 5:45). Common grace enables truth, virtue, and beauty to exist even in the absence of Christian faith, and those verities always stem from God, even without human acknowledgment or awareness. As Dante says of the preeminent Essence, or God, "any good / that lies outside of It is nothing but / a ray reflected from Its radiance."[3]

For the progressives, or neo-Calvinists, common grace "made many elements of human culture . . . not just products but *means* of grace, instruments whereby God restrained sin and enabled men [and women] to try to develop creation as he had originally designed."[4] John Calvin had spoken specifically about common grace's appearance in literature:

> Whenever we come upon these matters in secular writers, let that admirable light of truth shining in them teach us that the mind of man, though fallen, and perverted from its wholeness, is nevertheless clothed and ornamented with God's excellent gifts. If we regard the Spirit of God as the sole fountain of truth, we shall neither reject the truth itself, nor despise it wherever it shall appear.[5]

The traditionalists, on the other hand, emphasized Kuyper's concept of the antithesis—the total dichotomy between those who lived in relationship to God and those who denied God: "Since they embodied

3. Dante Alighieri, *Paradiso*, trans. Allen Mandelbaum (New York: Bantam, 1986), Canto XXVI, 34–36, p. 237.
4. James D. Bratt, *Dutch Calvinism in Modern America: A History of a Conservative Subculture* (Grand Rapids: Eerdmans, 1984), 20.
5. John Calvin, *Institutes of the Christian Religion*, ed. John T. McNeill (Philadelphia: Westminster, 1960), 1:273.

two different principles, they had no task in common and neither reason nor opportunity to cooperate."[6] Those who highlighted the antithesis were suspicious of society and culture, dissecting and condemning its failures, while the progressives thought their "task [was] not . . . to fan the antithesis into brighter burning but proclaim the well-meant divine disposition."[7] As I learned when I arrived in Grand Rapids, the *Reformed Journal* had been founded in 1951 by the progressives, who were now the dominant party at Calvin. My childhood had been spent in a traditionalist community, but I had been raised in what essentially amounted to a progressive home. Covenant was more of a traditionalist institution, especially in its departments of religion and philosophy. The contradictions and struggles, blessings and limitations, of my upbringing began to fall into place.

Literature Through the Eyes of Faith

Despite the fact that I was only in a one-year position, Calvin generously gave me a reduced teaching load in order to work on *Literature Through the Eyes of Faith*, which I had been asked to cowrite with Wheaton College's Roger Lundin, signaling Calvin's commitment to my development as a writer. The *Through the Eyes of Faith* series was designed to provide supplementary Christian textbooks for use in introductory college courses. Roger and I began our work reading literary theory together for several months because we thought it was essential to engage with the current state of our discipline, especially new claims about the nature of literary language, hermeneutics and conflicts of interpretation, and historical and contextual forces at work in and on literature. The few books addressing literature from a Christian perspective that were available for students didn't address these theoretical developments; they tended to advocate New Critical formalism, to identify archetypal and mythic patterns, to extol human creativity because it mirrored divine creativity, or to produce somewhat ponderous moralistic readings.

6. Bratt, *Dutch Calvinism*, 18.
7. James Daane, "The Principle of the Equal Ultimacy of Election and Reprobation," *Reformed Journal* 3 (November 1953): 15; cited in Bratt, *Dutch Calvinism*, 195.

Roger's forte was hermeneutical and historical issues, particularly what he viewed as the deleterious effect of Romanticism on our understanding of the nature of literature, while I was more concerned with presuppositional, canonical, and pedagogical issues. I knew by then that first- or second-year Christian college students had several basic questions about what literature was, why they should read literary works, and how they should go about reading such texts.

In the opening chapters of *Literature Through the Eyes of Faith*, Roger sets up the discussion historically and theoretically by demonstrating the false distinction between literary and scientific language that had been posited in an attempt to justify literature's existence and grant it authority, an authority that in the hands of first the Romantics and then the followers of Matthew Arnold became a substitute for religion. While some critics, such as Northrop Frye, extolled the exclusive power of literature to allow readers to flee reality for an imaginative world, Roger argues that literature "is neither an escape from reality nor a saving transformation of it. Instead, it enables us to respond to the order, beauty, and grace of God and his world and to the disorder that our sin has brought into that world."[8] Interpretation, metaphor, and narrative are God-given modes of human thought that help us construct meaning and live our lives, but literature does not hold a monopoly on those devices.

In later chapters, I consider literature's place within the biblical narrative of creation, fall, and redemption. Drawing on Wolterstorff's *Art in Action*, Calvin Seerveld's *Rainbows for a Fallen World*, and Henry Zylstra's *Testament of Vision*, I begin with God's role as the all-encompassing Creator to think about the what, the why, and the how of literature. In contrast to those who warily view human culture as an instance of the antithesis, who caution against human curiosity, citing the trouble produced by Eve's desire for knowledge, I argue that the Genesis story assigned humanity the task of developing the world of potential that the Creator-God had set into motion. Genesis 1:28, the creation mandate, reveals that the creation was not changeless perfection. Plants and trees bore fruit with seeds; birds and fish

---

8. Susan V. Gallagher and Roger Lundin, *Literature Through the Eyes of Faith* (San Francisco: Harper, 1989), xxix.

multiplied; human beings were "to fill" and "to work and take care" of God's world, beginning with the creative linguistic task of naming the animals. In unfolding the capacities of creation, humanity will produce science and technology; social, political, and economic structures; and art, music, and literature.

One way to fulfill the cultural mandate is through composing texts. A textual maker or author acts not as an omnipotent God-like creator, but rather as an imaginative improviser, bringing language, images, genres, forms, ideas, and emotions together in new configurations, simultaneously inspired and limited by his or her personal, social, and historical context. Literary compositions will undoubtedly show the effects of the fall in one way or another, but their production reflects faithful human activity.

The text that is produced becomes "literature" when a reader, typically within some kind of community, decides to read it as literature, following certain conventions and producing meaning through the act of reading. Thus, both writing and reading literature, creating and interpreting, are social practices, actions that are informed by the world and that, in turn, inform the world they enter. Graff explains how the act of reading is always contextual: "The initial questions we decide to ask in teaching a literary work, the questions that delimit what we will say about it, are always dictated in some part by the pressures of our time, our culture, and our sense of history: what is it in Shakespeare or Keats or Beckett that an age like ours . . . needs to relearn, consider imaginatively, or fight against?"[9] A literary text is neither object nor icon, but rather a generative site of action spooling out in countless directions, producing multiple meanings depending on the reader and the context, meanings that may well exceed, undercut, or even betray the author's original intention. Literature, in this definition, could be any text—written, visual, or aural—read as literature, with attention to its form, content, and context. The definitional lines are blurry, and that doesn't pose a problem; for example, Abraham Lincoln's commanding Second Inaugural Address could be read both as a historical document but also as a literary document,

9. Gerald Graff, *Professing Literature: An Institutional History* (Chicago: University of Chicago Press, 1987), 255.

with consideration of its rhetorical construction, allusions, and diction, along with its content and context.

Literature Through the Eyes of Faith, however, was written for first- or second-year college students, so despite its ontological arguments about the nature of literature and its hermeneutical affirmation of multiple interpretations, its main focus is on why and how we should read. Reading could be, I argue, one element of the Christian vocation, one way in which Christians could strive for shalom, toward forming a way of life in which we are in harmony with God, our neighbors, and the natural world. Reading works of great literature will not save people or automatically make them more humane, but reading literature is an effective and God-given way for Christians to explore, to love, and to delight in God's world. By imaginatively entering textual worlds, we can explore the height and depth and breadth of God's creation, encountering God in endlessly novel ways, since all creation was formed by God, was brought into being by Jesus Christ, and endures through the power of the Spirit. Dickinson's lyrical celebration of a gentian, Thoreau's translucent account of Walden, Herbert's shape-poem of an altar—they all help us to taste and see that the Lord is good.

Exploring God's good gifts in our reading includes both uncovering the mysteries of ourselves and meeting our neighbors across time and space. Exploration through reading can help us to love more fully, to cultivate our love of God and our neighbor in broader strokes. And it can result in delight as we savor the beauty, structure, insight, precision, or ambiguity of texts. In thinking about a Christian approach to literature, I draw on Wolterstorff's definition of shalom as encompassing aesthetic pleasures as well as social harmony, for literature's formal structures, artistic achievements, and creative heights are all essential. The Roman poet Horace famously said that the purpose of literature was "to delight and to instruct," and I argue that both enjoyment and edification are faithful acts for Christian readers.

The definition of literature and rationale for reading found in *Literature Through the Eyes of Faith* have substantial implications for selecting what to read. Working from God's creation of the world, human responsibility to cultivate its potential, and Christians' calling to advance shalom, I advocate for serious reconsideration of the pedagogical canon, arguing that works by women, American minorities, and world authors should become part of Christian college and university curricula.

Previous discussions of reading from a Christian perspective tended to emphasize Matthew Arnold's classicist model in which "the best that is known and thought in the world" was studied for its profound truth and wisdom, even though Arnold's "best" was limited to the white male Western world. Henry Zylstra, for example, opines, "The classics are precisely large and comprehensive human readings of life. They chart the course of the human spirit, and exhibit alternative answers to man's religious and philosophical quest."[10] Leland Ryken also presents a humanist defense of literature, which "puts us in touch with what is elemental and enduring and universal in human experience," and so "gives us forms for our feelings and our experiences of life."[11] The traditional canon dominated what Wolterstorff characterizes as "Stage II" of Christian liberal arts higher education, in which students were introduced to and taught "to interact fruitfully" with the "mighty stream" of high culture, including the great books of the Western tradition, in order to understand the human condition.[12] This pattern of thought highlights literature's expression of the universal, rather than the particular, and focuses on its capacity to help us improve ourselves rather than to love others. The traditional humanism endorsed by some Christian educators holds that reading literature somehow makes us better people, and the development of general education humanities requirements at the beginning of the twentieth century was based on that assumption.[13]

While not denying that both the universal and the self are important components of literature's exploration of God's world, I suggest that the historically inflected particulars of literature and insight into the lives of others are equally important for the Christian reader. Reading literature can help us to know and love our neighbor, a truth that is

10. Henry Zylstra, *Testament of Vision* (Grand Rapids: Eerdmans, 1958), 87–88.

11. Leland Ryken, ed., *The Christian Imagination: Essays on Literature and the Arts* (Grand Rapids: Baker, 1981), 123, 124.

12. Nicholas Wolterstorff, *Educating for Shalom: Essays on Christian Higher Education* (Grand Rapids: Eerdmans, 2004), 29, 267.

13. Jon H. Roberts and James Turner, *The Sacred and the Secular University* (Princeton: Princeton University Press, 2000).

simultaneously taught and embodied in Luke 10. When Jesus is challenged by a smart-aleck lawyer to explain what one should do to gain eternal life, he turns the question back on his interlocutor and asks what the Jewish Scriptures say. The educated lawyer can easily repeat the answer of the Torah: one must love God and love one's neighbor. "You have answered correctly," Jesus responds. "Do this and you will live" (v. 28). But the lawyer, since he *is* a smart aleck, retorts, "And who is my neighbor?" (v. 29). And as we all know, Jesus responds by telling a story, the story of the good Samaritan.

Stories can reveal our neighbors to us, as Jesus repeatedly demonstrates in his use of parables. Stories can jolt us out of our selfish preoccupations to consider another's life, the life of someone from a different culture, religion, gender, or class, in which the human differences are as striking as the universal similarities. If we want to encounter the full breadth of human life, God's grand quilt of human culture, the multiple human ways of striving for and expressing meaning, we will move beyond the traditional canon.

My reflections on what we should teach and read were occurring during the opening salvos of the "canon wars" in higher education. Allan Bloom's *The Closing of the American Mind*, with its lament for the loss of "the good old Great Books approach" was published in 1987,[14] and the infamous chant at Stanford University—"Hey hey, ho ho, Western culture's got to go"—took place in early 1988. My weighing of these academic debates was neo-Calvinist in terms of saying both yes and no, rejecting some arguments and accepting others, trying to identify the antithesis as well as the common grace.

The most radical opposition to the traditional canon, as epitomized in the Stanford chant, wanted to throw the entire tradition out, and I was not endorsing such an extreme position. The standard justification for studying the great tradition posited its aesthetic superiority, moral profundity, and enduring impact on Western society. I agreed that canonical texts are treasure chests of wisdom about what it means to be a human being, to struggle with evil and suffering, to live peacefully in community and the natural world, to acquire insight for life

14. Allan Bloom, *The Closing of the American Mind: How Higher Education Has Failed Democracy and Impoverished the Souls of Today's Students* (New York: Simon & Schuster, 1987), 334.

and death. Furthermore, the works of Shakespeare, Chaucer, Milton, Austen, Dickens, Hawthorne, Melville, James, Wharton, and others help us to understand Western culture and see ourselves within that culture, with both its strengths and its weaknesses. The classics sometimes affirm and other times challenge our deepest Christian values. (This was quite a different position than that held by Bloom, who believed that reading the classical texts would somehow discourage moral relativism.)

So while I did not advocate a wholesale rejection of the traditional canon, writing *Literature Through the Eyes of Faith* helped me to conceptualize the need to expand the study of literature radically. I had learned much from feminist and African American critics about relative standards of aesthetic judgment; of historical injustices of education, publication, and distribution; and of the value of recovering lost voices. One of the revelations of contemporary literary theory, particularly historical studies of publication and reception, was the contingent nature of the traditional canon. With no formal process of construction, the canon of so-called great works percolated from the critical and pedagogical work of white, upper-middle-class Western European men and was shaped by their preferences, assumptions, and judgments. Their dictates of "timelessness" and "universal greatness" were informed by their own subjective positions and often blind to other perspectives. Limited definitions of aesthetic quality impaired the reading and appreciation of texts in unfamiliar genres.

In the 1970s and 1980s, feminist and ethnic American scholars began documenting such biases, discovering forgotten texts, developing new means to assess them formally, and promoting their inclusion in standard anthologies and curricula. Noncanonical texts carried beauty and truth, as well as new voices and perspectives. If we believed that reading helped us to explore God's world, why would we limit that exploration to the world of the white men of the West? Might the realms of the sewing circle, chattel slavery, or reservation life be worth exploring also? If we believed that reading helped us to delight in and enjoy God's good gifts, why would we not learn how to appreciate the aesthetics of a different culture or genre? If we believed that reading could be one way in which we learned how to love our neighbors, why wouldn't we want to meet some neighbors from outside America, England, or Europe? Reading for shalom, I argue in *Literature Through the Eyes of Faith*, includes reading beyond the classics of the Western tradition, even though this means less coverage of classical texts, for additions to a course or curriculum necessitate the subtraction of something else.

The Anglo-European bias of the traditional canon meant that few Americans in the 1980s were reading works from Asia, South America, or Africa, even in courses with titles like "Masterpieces of World Literature," which focused on Western literature. For example, the *Norton Anthology of World Masterpieces*, originally published in 1956, issued a "companion volume," *Masterpieces of the Orient* in 1977, but did not add Asian, Middle Eastern, African, Caribbean, and Native American literature to its contents until 1995. The first major competition for Norton in the world literature market did not appear until 1984, with the publication of Prentice Hall's more accurately titled *Literature of the Western World*. An exclusive focus on the Western tradition of literature was not appropriate for Christians, I argued in a series of essays and talks; we needed to break out of our self-centered focus on our own nation, literature, and tradition to learn more about others. Our responsibility to promote justice, to address the needs of the oppressed, and to identify with the sorrowful should prompt us to read more widely.

In short, writing *Literature Through the Eyes of Faith* was an amazing gift for a faculty member in an early stage of her career. I was compelled to wrestle with the most rudimentary issues facing a would-be Christian literary scholar: defining *what* literature is; considering *why* I, as a Christian, should devote my life to reading, analyzing, and writing about literature; and judging *how* to do this kind of work. I had to identify and embrace my own theological moorings, working out the implications of my neo-Calvinist perspectives in relationship to contemporary movements in literary theory; I had to articulate the assumptions that would guide my future work.

Newer faculty seldom have the time or inclination to do this kind of extended intellectual work, given the experience of drinking from a fire hose that characterizes initial years in a full-time academic position. And such questions are not expected or encouraged during one's graduate school training. Most programs merely induct students into a discipline and form them as professionals, without much navel-gazing and certainly without asking theological questions. I know that Christian graduate students grapple with these issues in their hearts and minds and journals, and that a variety of support groups—such as InterVarsity, denominational campus ministries, and the Lilly Graduate Fellows program—aid in this process, but the discipline of articulating my position in an extensive piece of writing was, for me, a powerfully defining moment in my academic life, giving direction to both my future teaching and scholarship.

Writing for the Academy: A Story of South Africa

Following my trial year at Calvin, I took a tenure-track position in the English department, where I taught for the next six years. These are the years in which I became a scholar, building on the foundation of *Literature Through the Eyes of Faith* in my applied criticism, publishing my first three books, and changing my scholarly direction as I drifted away from American literature to work on issues originating in the South African literature course I had taught at Covenant.

Scholarship was respected at Calvin, and my colleagues across campus were writing essays and books, debating intellectual issues, and discussing Reformed thought. Calvin took teaching seriously, but it also provided reduced teaching loads, grants to support travel and research, student assistants, and administrative support—all of which made being a teacher-scholar much more feasible. The Calvin Center for Christian Scholarship was at the center of much of this support, and I served on its governing board for three years. I owe the fact that I am a scholar to the substantial support of Calvin during those seven years and to the blessings of my Reformed intellectual inheritance.

As I launched my scholarly career following *Literature Through the Eyes of Faith*, one of the first strategic issues I faced was the question of audience. For whom should I write: the church or the academy? The Christian college or the secular university? I enjoyed writing for a general audience, as in my journalistic past, but in the academic world, publishing in peer-reviewed scholarly journals and university presses was the gold standard. There were a handful of peer-reviewed

Christian journals, and several Christian publishers—such as Baker, Eerdmans, InterVarsity, and Zondervan—were potential venues, but at this point only Eerdmans published literary criticism, and those works were few and far between. The Catholic university presses, such as Notre Dame and Fordham, had not yet started extensive publishing programs, and Baylor University Press was basically just a regional Baptist organ.

In the late 1980s, I became part of an informal group of Christian scholars from several institutions who met each summer for a week to read literary theory, and we had heated debates about publishing strategies. Should we first establish ourselves as disciplinary scholars, earning a standing in the academy by producing solid academic work, before outing ourselves as Christian scholars or advancing more overtly Christian analyses and arguments? This seemed to have been the strategy adopted by some of the most successful Christian historians and philosophers. One member of our group vowed that he would never publish with a Christian publisher, because he wanted his work to be read by the critical establishment, not isolated in a Christian ghetto. Others felt that it was important to contribute to the handful of existing Christian scholarly journals in order to advance the cause of explicitly Christian scholarship. Some anticipated that only Christian publications would be receptive to the topics about which they wanted to write, and one published exclusively with Christian publishers and in Christian journals, not venturing into the secular publishing world until much later in his career.

As I pondered these options, I considered the way Nicholas Wolterstorff deliberately moved between two audiences: he published scholarly works with the best university presses and disciplinary journals but also explicitly Christian essays and books, some more academic and others written for the general public. *Works and Worlds of Art* (Oxford University Press, 1980), for example, had been complemented by *Art in Action: Toward a Christian Aesthetic* (Eerdmans, 1980).[15] While I had no illusions that I could achieve Wolterstorff's quality or quantity of scholarship, I intentionally decided to write for multiple

15. More recently, Wolterstorff's *Justice: Rights and Wrongs* (Princeton: Princeton University Press, 2008) was complemented by *Justice in Love* (Grand Rapids: Eerdmans, 2011).

audiences—secular and Christian, general readers and academic scholars. Since making that decision twenty years ago, I have published in a variety of academic journals, including *Contemporary Literature*, *Studies in the Novel*, and *Publications of the Modern Language Association of America* (PMLA), as well as *Christianity and Literature*, *Christian Scholars Review*, and *Christian Educators Journal*. Because *Literature Through the Eyes of Faith* was written for Christian college students and had been published by the religious division of Harper and Row, I resolved that my second book would be a scholarly work published by a university press.

That book decisively piloted me into southern waters. My initial foray into South African literature had piqued my interest in the work of J. M. Coetzee, but it also presented a pedagogical challenge: how to teach powerful, morally profound novels that include unsettling accounts of abuse and torture. That challenge led to a scholarly project—a conference paper that next became a journal essay on Coetzee's third novel, *Waiting for the Barbarians*.

Narrated by a courteous, learned man known only as the Magistrate, *Waiting for the Barbarians* is set in a small village on the frontier between an unnamed Empire and the wastelands inhabited by a nomadic tribe called the barbarians. When jackbooted Empire security forces arrive to investigate rumors of a barbarian attack, they interrogate and torture the few barbarians they manage to capture. The Magistrate is powerless to stop the abuse; however, he takes a barbarian woman, crippled because of her torture, into his house and bed as an act of contrition. Later, he makes an arduous journey across the desert to return the woman to her people. The imperial army arrives to fight the barbarians in his absence, and when the Magistrate returns, he is himself imprisoned for treason and tortured. Unable to locate the barbarians and decimated by guerilla attacks and the harsh desert conditions, the army abandons the village to its fate. Once again under the leadership of the Magistrate, the few remaining villagers wait for the barbarian hordes to descend in the ominous close of the novel.

Published in 1982, *Waiting for the Barbarians* won numerous international prizes, was selected as one of the best books of the year by the *New York Times*, and was heralded as a brilliant universal fable.

"The intelligence Coetzee brings us in *Waiting for the Barbarians* comes straight from Scripture and Dostoevsky," Webster Schott wrote. "We possess the devil. We are all barbarians."[16] But, as I discovered in teaching the novel, and as Coetzee himself reflected in the *New York Times Book Review* in 1986, the novel also posed troubling ethical questions for the author and readers alike: How can an author write about South Africa? Should a novel depict torture?

In his essay Coetzee described the moral dilemmas faced by a writer who depicts "the dark chamber." Writers in situations like South Africa should not ignore or hide the reality of state-sanctioned torture, he argues, but how can they represent torture without assisting the state in terrorizing people? Fictional accounts of torture also might produce a gratuitous fascination with gruesome details. Is there a middle ground between hiding and exposing atrocities?[17] As a reader, I wondered, could reading works of literature about "the dark chamber" contribute to shalom? On a more visceral level, this was the very question my students had raised. Why should we read this shocking book? So in writing about Coetzee, I examined the moral problem of depicting torture in a novel, describing Coetzee's formal solution of constructing *Waiting for the Barbarians* simultaneously as a vague (rather than precise) allegory and as a postmodern text of gaps and uncertainties. Rather than writing in the authoritative voice of an omniscient narrator or a powerful protagonist, Coetzee employs the narrative persona of a decent but weak man whose words and actions fail him and who ultimately realizes his own unwitting but undeniable complicity in the Empire's oppression. Rather than a romantic godlike narrator who constructs and rectifies the world through imagination and aesthetic achievement, *Waiting for the Barbarians* is recounted by an all-too-fallible human being who faces limits of language, custom, prejudice, and history. The power of the novel comes from the lack of power possessed by the narrator.

One thing led to another: I had initially read the novel in order to teach a course, and the pedagogical challenges that *Waiting for the Barbarians* raised and my commitment to shalom led me to write about

16. Webster Schott, "At the Farthest Outpost of Civilization," review of *Waiting for the Barbarians*, by J. M. Coetzee, *The Washington Post*, May 2, 1982.

17. J. M. Coetzee, "Into the Dark Chamber: The Novelist and South Africa," *New York Times Book Review*, January 12, 1986.

the novel. This, in turn, prompted me to research critical conversations in South African literature and Coetzee studies. With the exception of *Foe*, his fifth novel, all of Coetzee's work to this point alluded to South Africa, although often indirectly, and this presented problems for many critics who thought his work should be more overtly political. Given the official South African censorship system that banned many texts throughout the 1970s and 1980s, some wondered if Coetzee's ambiguity was pragmatically strategic.

Writers living in the apartheid state faced difficult questions: How far could they go in depicting South African oppression and still be published? Should they even write at all, or would political action be more appropriate? Should they produce works of art or acts of opposition? Could writing novels be an action against apartheid? The specific dilemma of the South African writer under apartheid in some ways epitomizes a question faced by all writers, including Christians, who feel a call and responsibility to work toward justice but want to maintain artistic integrity without producing mere propaganda. I saw Coetzee's novels as exploring innovative fictional strategies for engaging political as well as moral issues, and so I set out to demonstrate how his fiction did this in my first scholarly book, *A Story of South Africa: J. M. Coetzee's Fiction in Context* (1991).

The neo-Marxist critics dominating South African literary criticism in the 1980s were arguing that Coetzee's failure to depict contemporary South African events in realistic detail was an abrogation of historical responsibility.[18] American reviewers like Schott tended to read Coetzee's novels in terms of their universal qualities, as aesthetic objects that contained transcendent truths, with merely a brief nod to the South African context. Only one book-length study of Coetzee had been published in the United States at this point, a work that emphasized the universal: "Coetzee's fictions maintain their significance apart from a South African context, because of their artistry and because they transform urgent societal concerns into more enduring questions regarding colonialism."[19]

18. For example, Stephen Watson, "Colonialism and the Novels of J. M. Coetzee," *Research in African Literature* 17 (1986): 376.

19. Dick Penner, *Countries of the Mind: The Fiction of J. M. Coetzee* (Westport, CT: Greenwood, 1989), xiii.

A third perspective came from some Anglo-American academic critics who read Coetzee's fiction as a virtuoso linguistic exercise in meaninglessness: "We have arrived, as we often do in postmodern fiction, at a giving up, a frustration, a despair before the arbitrariness of language and its essential defectiveness for depicting the world. We have circled around again to the notion that language is a game, that the game is futile, that linguistic zero is ever-present."[20]

But working from a definition of literature as a form of action and social practice, I thought that Coetzee's novels could be read within the context of South Africa as innovative protests, neither vague universalism nor meaningless postmodernism. His works did raise universal issues of good and evil, oppression and justice, transcendence and historical contingency, but those universals were always rooted in concrete, specific South African situations by historical production as well as textual echoes. Both the metaphysical and the material, personal convictions and social rhetoric, contributed to oppression in the textual world that he fashioned.

My book involved extensive research into a variety of South African contexts, including colonial travel narratives; Afrikaner theology, mythology, and patriarchy; and the practice and rhetoric of torture. Not wanting to support the apartheid government by bringing American dollars into their economy, I opted to conduct my research in London, primarily in the majestic Reading Room of the British Library. The manuscript I initially submitted in the fall of 1990 before giving birth to my son analyzed Coetzee's first five novels, but when his sixth novel, *Age of Iron*, was published two months later, my publisher asked me to write an additional chapter, which I did in a fog of sleep deprivation between times of nursing.

Hoping to publish with a major university press, I made no explicitly Christian comments, although in the preface I briefly described my personal commitment to work for justice in South Africa as a member of the Christian Reformed Church, and I identified my critical perspective: "Operating from the premise that a literary text is both a product of human action and also a means whereby we as readers and critics perform certain other kinds of action, I aim to examine the

20. Lance Olsen, "The Presence of Absence: Coetzee's *Waiting for the Barbarians*," *Ariel* 16, no. 2 (1985): 55.

ethical implications of Coetzee's novel writing."[21] I was astonished and elated when Harvard University Press accepted the manuscript. This occurred because I happened to be writing about Coetzee at exactly the right time; although he was receiving positive reviews, only a few scholarly articles and two academic books on his work had appeared. The controversies over *Disgrace* (1999), Coetzee's immigration to Australia, and the 2002 Nobel Prize in literature were yet to come, along with his ongoing stream of publications. Within ten years of the appearance of *A Story of South Africa*, Coetzee was one of the most frequently written-about contemporary authors in the academy.

Postcolonial Literature and the Biblical Call for Justice

My next major project moved completely into the globe-encompassing world of non-Western literature and once again began inauspiciously with my saying yes to a small request. The Conference on Christianity and Literature (CCL), in which I had actively participated for several years, asked me to organize and chair a session on "Third-World Literature and the Biblical Call for Justice" at the 1990 Modern Language Association Convention. The CCL's use of the term *third world* was typical of the period. Although it had originally referred to those newly independent countries that were not aligned during the Cold War with either the West (the United States and its allies, including Commonwealth nations) or the East (Russia and China), *third world* later denoted any country with a high level of poverty and a lack of modern development.

To indicate the reality that the vast majority of the world lived in such conditions, some scholars preferred the term *two-thirds world*. B. R. Tomlinson astutely notes, "Like other collective descriptions of Africa, Asia, the Middle East, the Pacific islands and Latin America—such as the 'South', the 'developing world', or the 'less-developed world'—the designation 'Third World' was more about what such places were not than what they were."[22] After 1994, academic use of

---

21. Susan VanZanten Gallagher, *A Story of South Africa: J. M. Coetzee's Fiction in Context* (Cambridge, MA: Harvard University Press, 1991), xi.

22. B. R. Tomlinson, "What Was the Third World?," *Journal of Contemporary History* 38, no. 2 (2003): 307.

third world declined rapidly, with *postcolonial* or *global* becoming the preferred language.[23]

In fact, when I followed the suggestion of a university press editor who attended the MLA session to compile for publication a collection of essays on the topic, I changed the title to *Postcolonial Literature and the Biblical Call for Justice*. The discipline was moving quickly to embrace the study of international authors and literature, and I was scrambling to keep up. The premise of the volume was simple but unprecedented: then-current discussions of postcolonial literature were omitting or distorting a fundamental dimension of postcolonialism—namely, the role of Christianity in general and the biblical tradition in particular. Postcolonial literary theory was addressing topics such as the relationship of postcolonial literature and postmodernism, the influence and role of indigenous cultures, whether postcolonial writers should employ local or European languages, and the operations of cross-fertilization, hybridity, and mimicry. If Christianity or the Bible were mentioned in these discussions at all, they were typically seen as being identical to, in collusion with, or endorsing colonial oppression.

It was true that throughout Central and South America, Africa, and Asia, the colonial condition had been constructed by a complex blend of economic interests, ostensible moral superiority, and power politics—or "gold, God, and glory."[24] The "white man's burden" to transform indigenous religions, societies, and cultures often did mask or even sanction political control and economic exploitation. But belief in Western moral superiority, although often couched in religious terms, was not always explicitly or exclusively informed by Christianity. As moralistic imperialism became a surrogate faith for many in the modern age, racist ideology stemming from Darwinian evolution and secular humanism also contributed to such attitudes.[25] The human drive to find something to worship that so often re-

23. A keyword search of *third world* at the British Library in 2003 produced 1,805 books. "Of these, 140 were published before 1975, 654 between 1975 and 1984, 755 between 1985 and 1994, and 169 between 1995 and 2001" (ibid., 308).

24. Robin W. Winks, ed., *British Imperialism: Gold, God, Glory* (New York: Holt, 1963).

25. Philip Darby, *Three Faces of Imperialism: British and American Approaches to Asia and Africa 1870–1970* (New Haven: Yale University Press, 1987).

sulted in self-idolatry lay behind many colonial and imperialistic impulses.

While missionaries at times abetted colonization and, in some instances, wielded their own heavy-handed cultural imperialism, many also toiled to oppose colonial abuses and the excesses of their own religious bodies. They gave shelter to refugees; fed the hungry; mediated in internecine warfare; protested European commercial, military, and political cruelties; opposed female circumcision; and provided desperately needed medical care. The exceptional education provided by mission schools across South America, Asia, and Africa prepared future indigenous political leaders and fostered an entire generation of major new literary voices. Mission organizations conducted systematic studies of indigenous languages and literatures, sanctioning their worth and complexity.

Furthermore, Christian thought and rhetoric, particularly the call for justice articulated throughout the Scriptures, offered a countercultural voice against oppression, with the central biblical motif of liberation from Exodus serving as a controlling narrative for liberation movements throughout the world. The ethics of biblical justice buttressed many anticolonial movements and emerging postcolonial cultures. The twelve contributors to *Postcolonial Literature and the Biblical Call for Justice* discussed texts from Nicaragua, Colombia, Chile, Argentina, Nigeria, Kenya, South Africa, Egypt, and Palestine and drew on liberation, feminist, and neo-Calvinist theology's articulations of the Christian message of freedom, justice, and peace. The collection proposed innovative ways to talk about postcolonial literature, adding previously unrecognized voices to the ongoing critical conversation.[26]

When the manuscript for *Postcolonial Literature and the Biblical Call for Justice* was first submitted for publication, it did not include an essay on Chinua Achebe's *Things Fall Apart*, the most frequently taught postcolonial novel, one that directly engages with the impact of Christianity, missionary activities, and definitions of justice. When

26. The preceding discussion is adapted from my "Introduction: New Conversations on Postcolonial Literature," in *Postcolonial Literature and the Biblical Call for Justice*, ed. Susan VanZanten Gallagher (Jackson: University Press of Mississippi, 1994), 3–33.

the publisher pointed out that no discussion of postcolonial literature would be complete without consideration of Achebe's work, I
searched in vain for someone to write about *Things Fall Apart* and
ended up doing it myself.

The summer theory group had been appreciatively reading literary
theorist Mikhail Bakhtin, whose dialogical theory was indebted to
his Russian Orthodox faith, so I decided to see what insights a dialogical reading of *Things Fall Apart* might produce. Bakhtin's theory
provided rewarding ways to interpret postcolonial literature and to
think about the dynamics of a Western reader reading non-Western
literature. One of Bakhtin's central arguments was that dialogue is an
ongoing process that produces space for ethical action. A dialogical
text includes multiple voices in continual conversation, even though
many social and discursive practices attempt to impose an authoritative, monologic voice and to suppress or subordinate other voices.
Bakhtin saw the novel as an inherently dialogical form, and he much
preferred its heteroglossia to what he saw as the monological genres
of poetry or epic. The world of *Things Fall Apart* reverberates with
voices, both within indigenous Igbo society and among the different
Westerners who come to Igboland with vastly opposing motives and
behaviors. Achebe's text does not portray a simple black-and-white
dichotomy between the Igbo and the British, but finds weaknesses
and strengths in each, says both yes and no, particularly with respect
to ideas about justice.[27]

Bakhtin also considers dialogue's role in the process of interacting
with a culture other than one's own, and his theories helped me think
more about how Western readers might approach African texts in a
way that supports fashioning a world of justice and peace. Learning to
know the other, according to Bakhtin, should be a dialogical process,
not an objective fact-gathering mission or a purely subjective gut-level
response. When Western readers first encounter postcolonial texts,
they often attempt to cultivate a sympathetic identification: "There
exists a very strong, but one-sided and thus untrustworthy, idea that
in order better to understand a foreign culture, one must enter into

27. For a full discussion, see my "The Dialogical Imagination of Chinua Achebe,"
in *Postcolonial Literature and the Biblical Call for Justice*, 136–51.

it, forgetting one's own, and view the world [entirely] through the eyes of this foreign culture."[28] C. S. Lewis, for example, says, "We want to see with other eyes, to imagine with other imaginations, to feel with other hearts, as well as with our own. . . . My own eyes are not enough for me, I will see through those of others."[29]

Lewis's dictum to "empty our minds and lay ourselves open," to think, as it were, like an Igbo, is mistaken, says Bakhtin. A Dutch-American woman can never see African life as an Igbo does. But the opposite tack—claiming "the Igbo people are just like us," glossing over differences in order to emphasize the universal—also distorts perception and produces misunderstanding. What I might view as universal could very well be a product of my own culture and perspective. Both approaches demonstrate "the false tendency toward reducing everything to a single consciousness, toward dissolving in it the other's consciousness."[30] Instead, as we read postcolonial literature, our goal should be "creative understanding" through dialogue:

> *Creative understanding* does not renounce itself, its own place in time, its own culture; and it forgets nothing. In order to understand, it is immensely important for the person who understands to be *located outside* the object of his or her creative understanding—in time, in space, in culture. For one cannot even really see one's own exterior and comprehend it as a whole, and no mirrors or photographs can help; our real exterior can be seen and understood only by other people, because they are located outside us in space and because they are *others*.[31]

We remain ourselves, but we listen respectfully and with openness to the expressions of others. A dialogic reading of postcolonial literature, then, does not result in a simple synthesis of ideas, nor even in a dialectical resolution, but rather in a mutual enrichment. Dialogue helps us recognize truths about ourselves that we did not previously see, as well as generate previously untapped truths from others: "[In]

28. Mikhail M. Bakhtin, *Speech Genres and Other Late Essays*, trans. Vern W. McGee, ed. Caryl Emerson and Michael Holquist (Austin: University of Texas Press, 1986), 6–7.

29. C. S. Lewis, *An Experiment in Criticism* (Cambridge: Cambridge University Press, 1961), 137, 140.

30. Bakhtin, *Speech Genres*, 141.

31. Ibid., 7.

a dialogic encounter of two cultures . . . each retains its own unity and *open* totality, but they are mutually enriched."[32]

A dialogical approach cultivating creative understanding also has significant implications for thinking about the canon, as Morson and Emerson explain: "The great texts of any culture require the perspective of other cultures to develop their potential."[33] Reading about other cultures will not only assist us in understanding those cultures but it will also help us see Western literature differently, as we approach it from other cultural perspectives, with different questions and presuppositions. What happens when we read the masterpieces of the great tradition in new ways, working from an African context?

When Achebe read Joseph Conrad's classic *Heart of Darkness*, he saw "a story in which the very humanity of black people is called in question," in which Africans are dehumanized by being portrayed as ignorant, speechless, irrational savages, despite the novel's exposure and condemnation of colonial exploitation and brutality.[34] Achebe insists that Conrad's intended compassion for Africans does not excuse his narrative failure to treat them respectfully as human beings. And to the contextual defense that Conrad's racial insensitivity was merely typical for his time, Achebe provides the counter examples of David Livingstone and Thomas Gainsborough.[35] One can never again read *Heart of Darkness* in the same way after contemplating Achebe's cogent and disturbing argument.

Reconsideration of the Western canon need not always be as controversial as Achebe's reading of Conrad. Recent work in Shakespeare studies, for example, has contextualized *The Tempest* and *Othello* in light of the global exploration of the sixteenth century, leading to provocative and fresh insights. Other scholars have considered the ways in which Shakespeare's plays have, or have not, been effectively translated into other languages and cultures, putting the issue of their

32. Ibid.

33. Gary Saul Morson and Caryl Emerson, *Mikhail Bakhtin: Creation of a Prosaics* (Stanford: Stanford University Press, 1990), 289.

34. Chinua Achebe, "An Image of Africa: Racism in Conrad's *Heart of Darkness*," in *Heart of Darkness*, by Joseph Conrad, ed. Robert Kimbrough, 3rd ed. (New York: Norton, 1988), 259.

35. Chinua Achebe, *The Education of a British-Protected Child: Essays* (New York: Knopf, 2009), 90–91.

universality to the test. Why is *King Lear* so popular in Japan and China? Why did the Zulu version of *Macbeth*, *Umabatha*, written in 1970 and performed throughout Africa, England, and the United States for over forty years, prompt Peter Ustinov to say that, until he saw *Umabatha*, he did not truly understand *Macbeth*?[36] Why do African audiences have such difficulty with *Hamlet*?

In such discussions, it is sometimes tempting to cast "the West" as the perceiving agent and "the rest" of the world as merely the object of recognition, to read non-Western literature exclusively in light of Western literature, or, as Achebe puts it, "to set Africa up as a foil to Europe."[37] Too often Anglo-European readings glibly become binary oppositions of "us" and "them," instead of more nuanced affirmations, disagreements, exchanges, and embraces. True polyphonic dialogue among North and South, Europeans and Africans, is challenging. As Achebe points out, one cannot simply talk about "cultural exchange in a spirit of partnership between North and South," because "no definition of partnership can evade the notion of equality."[38] The history of Western expansion and colonialism has established an asymmetrical situation in which one voice has continually subdued or dismissed the other. Given that history, Western readers should be more proactive about and willing to listen to the voices of postcolonial people. The clashes of colonialism, Christianity, and Igbo traditionalism need to be considered from African as well as Western perspectives if we wish to love and deal justly with our fellow human beings.[39]

The Limits of Calvin College

While my seven years at Calvin helped me to recognize, articulate, and deepen my theological and educational stance as a neo-Calvinist

36. Donald G. McNeil Jr., "A New Stage for South Africa," *The New York Times*, July 6, 1997, http://www.nytimes.com/1997/07/06/theater/a-new-stage-for-south-africa.html?pagewanted=all. I was fortunate enough to see a production of *Umabatha* in Natal, South Africa, in 1995.

37. Achebe, "Image of Africa," 251.

38. Chinua Achebe, *Hopes and Impediments: Selected Essays* (New York: Doubleday, 1989), 22, 23.

39. See my "Reading and Faith in a Global Community," *Christianity and Literature* 54 (2005): 323–42.

and provided remarkable support for my growth as a scholar, those years also brought frustrations and disappointments. I had been able to teach two interim (January) courses in South African literature, but the English department of this era consistently resisted adding courses to the regular curriculum that ventured outside the traditional canon. When I suggested renaming the required World Literature course as, more accurately, Western Literature, no one listened. When I proposed a Literature by Women course, I was told that the excellent women writers were already in the canon, despite the fact that the then-current Great American Novel course didn't include any women or African American writers. I was accused of playing identity politics rather than adhering to the universal aesthetic judgments of the canon. If we let in some women authors "just because they were women," what would be next? Homosexual writers? Although I genuinely respected the kindly older male professor who said this to me, it was not his finest moment.

Furthermore, I had begun to read more widely in African literature, and I wanted to teach some of these absorbing, challenging, and wonderful texts to encourage my students to think more broadly about the world. But there was no way I could get a course in African literature into the curriculum. I felt increasingly alienated from my department; there were only two other full-time women English professors, neither of whom had small children,[40] and I had learned that many of the most significant departmental issues were debated and resolved in the men's locker room after racquetball games.

I did have other close female friends from other parts of campus, meeting weekly with a small faculty prayer group who also mentored me in motherhood, and I had become deeply invested in the congregational life of Church of the Servant, where I encountered genuine support for women and the spiritual sustenance of liturgical worship. After further prayer, study, and reflection, as well as meeting several women experiencing God's call to the ministry in their own lives, I had come to believe that both men and women were called to serve in church ministry positions. But the seemingly endless denominational

40. A third woman, Susan Felch, joined the department during my last year at Calvin.

battles over the role of women in the Christian Reformed Church were wearisome and demoralizing. I appreciated the Reformed tradition and would always identify myself as part of it, but I was ready to swim in the larger ocean of Christian academic life.

There were pulls as well as pushes in my decision to leave Calvin for Seattle Pacific University (SPU). My son was now almost three years old, and all of my family lived in Washington. I wanted him to grow up knowing his grandparents, aunts, uncles, and cousins, even if he didn't spend every Sunday afternoon eating ham buns with them. My husband, originally from Los Angeles, was eager to return to the West, missing the mountains, the Pacific Ocean, and the rugged individualism. Seattle was a scenic, progressive, culturally vibrant city, with a Thai restaurant and coffee shop seemingly on every other block. And SPU wanted me to develop an African literature course, teach a long-established Ethnic American literature course, and work to revise the English curriculum to be more international and multicultural. So in an abysmal instance of academic timing, immediately after having been recommended for tenure by the Calvin English department, I submitted my resignation, and our family moved to Seattle in 1993.

❖ 4 ❖

The Pacific

1993–2000

In *Moby-Dick*, when Ishmael arrives at the Pacific Ocean after several months of sailing, he writes, "Now the long supplication of my youth was answered; that serene ocean rolled eastwards from me a thousand leagues of blue."[1] Except for the fact that the magnificent Puget Sound rolled westward from Seattle, I felt Ishmael's joy, for the long supplication of two decades had at last resulted in a return to my treasured Pacific Northwest.

No move, no matter how welcome, is without its disadvantages, and Seattle Pacific's quarter system (rather than semesters), uneven administrative leadership, and lack of support for scholarship were among those I faced, but SPU's English department was cordial, creative, and thriving. The university went through three different presidents during my first three years there, but my department worked without animosity to construct a new English major in which students were required to take courses in British, American, and world literature—with

1. Herman Melville, *Moby-Dick; Or, The Whale* (Indianapolis: Bobbs-Merrill, 1964), 613.

81

the latter category reflecting the true diversity of the world.[2] I soon was offering a regular course in African literature. Across campus, I worked with other women faculty to establish SPU's first maternity leave policy and a Women's Studies minor, and the English department was happy to support the new program by adding a course in literature by women.

Teaching African Literature

In finally teaching an African literature course, I was able to draw together many ideas that I had developed over the past eleven years. The goals of this course included understanding the rich diversity and complex history of African literature across the continent; studying the themes and literary techniques of several works in depth, with general knowledge of other African writers; and considering the impact of Christianity upon African literature and the impact of African literature upon Christianity. Given my belief that literature is always enmeshed in life—both in its formation and its impact—the course also included a brief survey of African history. I wanted the students to learn more about Africa and its people in order to explore God's world and meet more of their neighbors. Reading African literature, I believed, would help them learn a lot about others as well as a little about themselves, providing both a window and a mirror. The course would address literary techniques, strategies, and achievements; trace the development of African literature through the pre-conquest, colonial, and postcolonial eras; and examine the contributions of indigenous forms, the Western realistic novel, postmodernism, and the hybridity that characterizes all post-independence literature.

African Literature opened with the rich heritage of oral literature that has been sung and recited on the African continent for thousands of years. In folk tales, proverbs, praise songs, love poems, and epics, oral literature provided entertainment at communal gatherings, celebrated great rulers and warriors, instructed children and

2. I'm sorry to say that this curricular structure no longer exists, although the African literature course is still offered regularly, and I will once again teach it in the fall of 2013.

youth, preserved history and lineages, and formed cultural identity. We read sections from the great Zulu epic *Shaka the Great*, and students struggled every bit as much to learn how to read and appreciate this text as they did with the *Odyssey* and *Beowulf*. However, the shared human elements of love, birth, death, war, revenge, suffering, salvation, and the transcendent, as well as specific cultural practices and expressions, eventually gripped them. The insight into reading and appreciating the form and aesthetics of oral literature that I gained from Professor Foley at Emory now stood me in good stead.

We then examined the ongoing oral traditions of praise poetry and occasional song, but also traced the ways in which African orature provides a foundation for many contemporary African texts. African writers often recount soaking in the magic of language and the power of narrative from their childhood immersion in nightly participatory storytelling around the fire in the family compound, and both thematic and formal influences from folk tales, myths and legends, historical chronicles, and epics permeate the subsequent written tradition.

A key historical context that we considered was the partition of the African continent among the European powers at the infamous Berlin Conference of 1884, where so many arbitrary borderlines were created, leading to huge questions of identity and future internal African conflicts. In Nigeria, for example, Britain triumphed over France by grabbing two protectorates around the Niger River: the North and the South. The North was primarily made up of Hausa-Fulani, who were Muslim and hierarchically ruled by emirs who collected taxes for the British. The South had many people groups, with the Yoruba dominating the Southwest and the Igbo the Southeast. The Igbo lived in small republican communities and were hard-working, ambitious traders. They were quickly Christianized, recognizing the practical and spiritual value in the life promoted by the missionaries. But the British had to create an artificial and quickly corrupted system of "warrant chiefs" since the Igbo had no centralized political power structures. In 1914, the British governor-general joined these religiously, socially, and culturally disparate people into a single protectorate called Nigeria. The arbitrary lines drawn around the Niger by cigar-smoking politicians in Brussels had long-lasting ramifications that often are found in Nigerian literature.

When we moved from orature to written texts, we began by acknowledging the distorted representations of Africans in earlier European texts, reading Achebe's essay on *Heart of Darkness* in order to understand how important it was for Africans to write their own accounts, to define themselves as complex human beings. With the literacy and education provided through mission organizations, followed by post–World War II independence, African novelists addressed colonial oppression and liberation themes, explored the suppressed riches of indigenous cultures, celebrated newly emerging national identities, and "wrote back" to earlier versions of Africa depicted in works such as Rider Haggard's *She* (1887), Conrad's *Heart of Darkness* (1899), or Joyce Cary's *Mister Johnson* (1939).

Achebe notes that his composition of *Things Fall Apart* originated in his desire to look at African life "from the inside," to demonstrate the profundity and complexity of Igbo culture not only to European readers but also to his own people: "I would be quite satisfied if my novels did no more than teach my [African] readers that their past— with its imperfections—was not one long night of savagery from which the first Europeans acting on God's behalf delivered them."[3] When Achebe published *Things Fall Apart* in 1958, Nigeria did not yet exist as an independent political state, so we discussed the significance of his writing a novel about African identity during the independence struggle. Achebe, fellow Nigerian dramatist Wole Soyinka, and Kenya's prolific Ngũgĩ wa Thiong'o are the three best-known African authors of the twentieth century, and we read all three. When Soyinka became the first post-independence African writer to win the Nobel Prize in literature in 1986, I told my students, African literature had unmistakably achieved a place in the canon of world literature.

After reading the "Big Three" and their accounts of colonialism, the role of Christianity, indigenous culture, and African identity, the class began to glimpse African literature's diversity. But I then tried to complicate matters further by introducing some lesser-known but equally gifted women writers, who provided other voices and perspectives. While *Things Fall Apart* set a powerful exemplar for

3. Chinua Achebe, *Hopes and Impediments: Selected Essays* (New York: Doubleday, 1989), 45.

future African writers, it had blind spots, particularly when it came to the role of Igbo women, who are depicted "as mere objects circulated among their menfolk . . . and systematically excluded from the political, the economic, the judicial, and even the [discursive] life of the community."[4] Furthermore, despite the fact that Achebe criticizes some aspects of Igbo society, such as its practice of twin infanticide, he doesn't disparage its treatment of women or its view of women's roles: "The women . . . are content with their lot. In their silence they assent to their status as the property of a man and to their reduction to a level lower than a barn full of yams in their role as signifiers of their husbands' wealth. So, too, does Achebe. For although he exposes, through the defection of *osu*, the injustice of Umuofia's social class system, he remains silent (mute like his women) on its gender hierarchy."[5]

The 1970s and 1980s witnessed the beginning of a female tradition in African fiction, with authors such as Grace Ogot, Flora Nwapa, Buchi Emecheta, and Mariama Bâ, who began "writing back" both to the empire and to the male African tradition. In the course, we read one novel by an African woman, and then each student worked independently on another woman author—gathering background information, studying her country's history, analyzing the text's themes and techniques, and finally presenting the class with an introduction to the novel. Since I knew the most about South African literature, and American college students remain especially intrigued by this country, the final third of the course treated South African literature by English, Afrikaans, and indigenous black writers.

A key principle underlying the entire course was the need to avoid simple dichotomies—a cohesive one-voiced "African" tradition versus the Western tradition. Certainly there were common elements, but writers from Nigeria, Kenya, Zimbabwe, and South Africa had different stories to tell; Christians and Muslims had different stories to tell; African men and women had different stories to tell. African literature is a polyphony as well as a discernible tune. Each voice was irremediably unique yet inextricably connected to others.

4. Florence Stratton, *Contemporary African Literature and the Politics of Gender* (London: Routledge, 1994), 25.
5. Ibid., 35.

During my years of teaching African literature, I found that one aspect of African life that especially impressed my students was the strong communal bonds extending beyond one's immediate family, the way in which an African person saw himself or herself in terms of relationships rather than solely through a sense of personal identity. In traditional African society, this understanding of the self is epitomized by the word *ubuntu*, a form of which appears in several different African languages. A popular Xhosa proverb advises, "*Ubuntu ungamntu ngabanye abantu*": "People are people through other people." Archbishop Desmond Tutu explains, "In the African *Weltanschauung*, a person is not basically an independent, solitary entity. A person is human precisely in being enveloped in the community of other human beings, in being caught up in the bundle of life. To be . . . is to participate."[6]

Nothing captures the sense of being enveloped in a community, caught up in the bundle of life, so well as the genre of the novel, and African *bildungsroman*, novels about growing up, were especially powerful texts for my students who were in the process of growing up themselves, trying to discern the proper boundaries and connections between themselves and their families and communities. American Christians could learn much about human ties and interdependence from African literature, which testified to the power, compassion, and necessity of such connections in a way not found in traditional American literature, which makes a hero out of the solitary Thoreau at Walden rather than recognizing the Thoreau who brought his dirty laundry to Mrs. Emerson each week.

I continued to teach Coetzee's *Waiting for the Barbarians*, but as I read more South African works, I felt compelled to write about some of the lesser-known literary voices from this remarkable country. The next logical step in my career, if a national reputation as a scholar had been my goal, would have been to do further work on Coetzee. During the 1990s, Coetzee steadily published novels, memoirs, essays, and criticism while his international stature soared, and I was (and still am) periodically asked to evaluate scholarship on his work for

6. Quoted in Antjie Krog, *Country of My Skull: Guilt, Sorrow, and the Limits of Forgiveness in the New South Africa* (New York: Random, 1998), 143.

academic journals and presses. However, one of the joys of being a professor at a Christian university without the rigorous scholarly expectations and pressures so common to research institutions was the ability to stray from the traditional academic career path. I had the freedom to select scholarly projects based on my passions rather than on the necessity for keeping up a steady pattern of publication. Of course, the downside of such freedom was that such scholarship would take longer to produce because of the lack of institutional support, especially at SPU as compared to Calvin.

Confession in South African Literature

The astonishing South African transition to democracy initiated in 1990 generated intriguing questions about the role of literature in the post-apartheid era, both in terms of the value of older protest works and the direction of recent national works. As I read more South African texts and watched unfolding events, one religiously tinged word cropped up repeatedly: *confession*. But this term was employed in a variety of seemingly incompatible contexts: prisoners in South Africa had been tortured to produce confessions, authors in South Africa wrote confessional autobiographies in the tradition of Saint Augustine, Christians in South Africa repeated liturgical confessions of faith and personal confessions of sin, the Reformed Church in South Africa issued a *status confessionis* condemning the theological justification of apartheid. These different kinds of confession—judicial, autobiographical, and theological—permeated South African literature from 1948 to the present.

I decided that I wanted to study the phenomenon of confession, identifying both historical practices and literary instances in an attempt to understand its purpose, value, and impact. My initial premise was that Christians saw confession as an indispensable, constructive activity; as created human beings we had a duty to confess—to God's sovereignty and mighty deeds as well as to our own sins and inadequacies. True confession was good for the soul and the community; false confessions damaged both individuals and societies. Might there similarly be beneficial and harmful literary confessions?

Thus, in designing this project, I began with a literary phenomenon, one that no other scholar had noticed or treated, and then identified the assumptions and resources the Christian tradition provided for analyzing the phenomenon and producing interpretations.

However, without much institutional support for scholarship at SPU, I needed to be more creative in finding time for research and writing. The university did not even have funding for regular faculty sabbaticals; departmental faculty had to take on extra loads to cover courses or drop a course from the curriculum for a year, making someone's sabbatical a burden on the rest of the department or an inconvenience for the students. Some faculty postponed or never even took sabbaticals out of a sense of duty toward their students, curriculum, and programs.

Calvin had an excellent Academic Research Grant Program that provided a faculty member with a full semester off from teaching in order to work on a scholarly project, but SPU offered only a handful of faculty grants that, at most, funded a one-course teaching reduction. Furthermore, the relentless pace of the quarter system made it difficult to sustain scholarly activity during the academic year. At both institutions I taught seven courses annually, but Calvin's 3-1-3 load distributed over two semesters and a January term was much more conducive to writing and research than SPU's 2-2-3 load, with brief ten-week terms and three time-consuming periods of start-up, advising, and finals. The solution to this difficulty was clear: I needed to find outside funding, so during my first years at SPU I repeatedly applied for the few national grants available for literary scholars.

After several rejections, I received not one but two fellowships that allowed me to take a year off from teaching, provided funding for my department to replace me, and supported my traveling to and spending several months in South Africa. Little did I know when I was putting these grant applications together that they would enable me to witness firsthand one of the most effective yet controversial displays of public confession in the twentieth century. I was blessed to receive both a Pew Evangelical Scholars Initiative (PESI) fellowship and a grant from the National Endowment for the Humanities.

Over the nine-year period of the PESI program, more than $4 million was awarded to more than one hundred scholars in theology, humanities, or the social sciences, and this program had a huge impact on the burgeoning of Christian scholarship in North America. Projects were to be influenced by Christian thought and to result in the publication of a significant book with a major university press. A white paper assessing the final results of the PESI found that about 75 percent of the projects resulted in such a publication.[7] In my PESI application, I proposed to research the historical development of religious and literary confession, specific practices of confession in South Africa, and several South African texts that depicted or employed confession. In a providential conjunction of events, I also was selected to participate in a National Endowment for the Humanities Summer Seminar on South African literature, held in South Africa in 1996. Following the seminar, I remained in South Africa for several months to travel and conduct research for both my book on confession and future work on Alan Paton. The summer of 1996 was especially eventful in South Africa as the country was mesmerized by the public hearings of the Truth and Reconciliation Commission, in which the practice of confession took front and center stage.

Because of my Christian rearing and education, I was particularly attuned to the language and practice of confession; like a dog that can hear a high-pitched tone imperceptible to people, I found instances of confession in a wide variety of sources. As a believer, I knew confession was a life-affirming action involving both testimony and admission, and as a literary scholar who specialized in the novel, I was aware of the long connection between confession and the development of the novel.[8] A widespread discursive and rhetorical practice, confession had originated in a Christian sacramental ritual that evolved into a judicial act and a literary form. In its theological origins, a confession is the act of speaking the truth in such a way as to acknowledge a debt, both by testifying to the actions of those who have provided help and by admitting to one's own shortcomings or

7. Michael S. Hamilton, "An Analysis of the Pew Programs in Support of Evangelical Scholarship, 1990–2004," unpublished paper, 2008. Hamilton notes, "By comparison, one study of scholars who received NEH [National Endowment for the Humanities] grants found that 45% of their Fellows published books within six years" (7).

8. The following discussion is adapted from my *Truth and Reconciliation: The Confessional Mode in South African Literature* (Portsmouth, NH: Heinemann, 2002).

failures. Confession is performative—doing something, not merely saying something. However, the confessional act, like everything else in creation, has fallen prey to sin; testimonies inscribe atrocities as well as gifts, humanity's sinful nature entails admissions of fault, and false confessions convey untruths, promote a narcissistic self, or fail to admit indebtedness and culpability.

Two eminent theorists—Michel Foucault and Mikhail Bakhtin—discuss confession in sharply conflicting terms, and their accounts set the parameters for my own analysis of confession's performance in South African literature. Foucault regards confession as an inevitably oppressive act, a means of exerting power over others, part of the disciplinary regime of modern culture; Bakhtin, on the other hand, sees confession as a way to affirm and promote the mutually dependent existence of self and other.

The thirteenth-century establishment of sacramental confession, according to Foucault, made confession "one of the West's most highly valued techniques for producing truth," a technique that was transplanted into the political and psychological realms.[9] Confession is not a "natural" way of arriving at truth, he argues; we have been conditioned to the degree that "the obligation to confess is now relayed through so many different points, is so deeply ingrained in us, that we no longer perceive it as the effect of a power that constrains us."[10] That power is wielded by the one who listens: "The confession is a ritual of discourse . . . that unfolds within a power relationship, for one does not confess without the presence . . . of a partner who is not simply the interlocutor but the authority who requires the confession, prescribes and appreciates it and intervenes in order to judge, punish, forgive, console and reconcile."[11] The modern self thus is socially constructed by the repressive power exerted in the discourse of confession.

In his emphasis on the confessor's authority and power, Foucault implies that the confessant is always an innocent victim. Certainly coerced judicial confessions made under duress or as a result of torture exemplify such victimization, but what about the confessant who

9. Michel Foucault, *The History of Sexuality*, trans. Robert Hurley (New York: Vintage, 1978–80), 3:59.
   10. Ibid., 1:60.
   11. Ibid., 1:61.

has actually committed an abhorrent act? Or what about the case of an innocent person who has been unjustly imprisoned and is only released when the real perpetrator confesses the truth? And what about confessions made in communal settings, such as the church, in which admitting guilt and testifying to God's goodness leads to an individual's flourishing and incorporation into a healthy community? Foucault's insights are valuable for helping us understand the perversions of confession—whether in torture chambers or on television reality shows—but they do not tell the whole story.

Bakhtin argues that the rhetoric of confession and its practice within a particular community reveals the dialogical nature of the self: the way in which the self always exists in relationship to others. The confessional act affirms this mutually dependent existence of self and other. Bakhtin also connects confession and literature, writing about Dostoevsky's novels, "He depicts confession and the confessional consciousnesses of others . . . in order to show the interdependence of consciousness that is revealed during confession. I cannot manage without another, I cannot become myself without another; I must find myself in another by finding another in myself."[12] Such mutual connections are one of the essences of the human being created in the image of the perichoretic Triune God. Theologian Miroslav Volf explains, "The human self is formed not through a simple rejection of the other—through a binary logic of opposition and negation—but through a complex process of 'taking in' and 'keeping out.' We are who we are not because we are separate from the others who are next to us, but because we are both separate and connected, both distinct and related."[13] Confession makes both such distinctions and such connections possible. In theological terms, confession comprises not a complete renunciation of the self but rather a decentering and subsequent recentering of the self within the community of faith. Properly practiced, confession fashions genuinely flourishing individual and communal identities.

This understanding of both the negative and the positive aspects of confession gave me the interpretive tools with which to examine

12. Mikhail Bakhtin, *Problems of Dostoevsky's Poetics*, ed. and trans. Caryl Emerson (Minneapolis: University of Minnesota Press, 1984), 287.

13. Miroslav Volf, *Exclusion and Embrace: A Theological Exploration of Identity, Otherness, and Reconciliation* (Nashville: Abingdon, 1996), 66.

instances of confession found in literature. I developed a theory of
"the confessional mode" as a narrative first-person account in which
a speaker expresses the need both to testify and to admit guilt about
particular events in order to reconstruct a self within community. The
confessional mode appears in fiction and nonfiction, printed texts
and oral discourse, and the poetry and prose of both apartheid-era
and post–apartheid-era narratives. While the confessional mode is
not unique to South Africa, its prominence there can be explained
by South African history, in which many voices had been systematically silenced by apartheid, in which coerced confessions dominated
the public consciousness for three decades, in which confession had
a significant religious presence, and in which, following the creation
of a democratic government, a new communal identity needed to be
formed in the face of heart-wrenching truths.

Writing about Coetzee's novels had been primarily an intellectual
exercise, a way to piece together the subtle connections among historical events, previous texts, and Coetzee's fantastical, self-reflexive
narratives. His fiction was strangely haunting, profoundly evocative, disturbingly commanding in the issues it raised and questions it
posed, but his protagonists tended to be idiosyncratic intellectuals,
captivating but somewhat distant beings. Several of Coetzee's novels
were confessional in terms of having a first-person narrator, like the
Magistrate, who recounted past events and admitted to shortcomings. But I turned now to autobiographical confessional texts, which
articulated the thoughts and emotions of historical South Africans
who had suffered unbelievable treatment. Their testimonies were at
times almost unendurable yet nonetheless revealed a miraculous faith
and endurance at which I could only marvel.

One section of my book *Truth and Reconciliation* treated autobiographies written by former political prisoners who had been tortured
because of their opposition to the apartheid state. South African
prisoners often underwent Foucauldian confession as they were psy-
chologically and physically pressured to admit to crimes or declare
themselves terrorists. They emerged from such experiences with a
deep psychological need to remake the self that had been destroyed
through penal confession, to reexamine truth in light of their experiences—to produce, as Breyten Breytenbach calls his account, "true

confessions."[14] After repeated demands for confession, most prisoners gave in, linguistically constructing themselves as demanded by their interrogators. Later, they needed to remake their shattered identity. The confessions of former prisoners—made in memoirs, speeches, films, or interviews—were therapeutic and recuperative by practicing confession as a voluntary, positive, self- and community-building act. Those of South African Christians were especially resonant, as one example will demonstrate.

The True Confession of a Pastor

Diary from a South African Prison, by Tshenuwani Simon Farisani, speaks with a spiritual anguish like that of Job, David, and the crucified Christ. Farisani was born in the northern Transvaal and became a Christian when he was twelve. He studied theology in Natal in the 1970s, where he was influenced by Steve Biko and the Black Consciousness Movement. Ordained as an Evangelical Lutheran pastor in 1979, Farisani was assigned a church in Venda, a newly formed "homeland," or *Bantustan*. Here he became a popular evangelist criticizing the apartheid-supported government and proclaiming a God of justice and love. For these activities, he was arrested and detained on three occasions, undergoing appalling torture during what he calls his "times in the bowels of hell." His book reports these experiences, but transforms the private account suggested by the word *diary* into a communal narrative: "In one small sense this is a personal story," the preface explains, "but in another wider, more realistic sense it is South Africa's tragic story."[15]

Religious language, images, and questions continually emerge as Farisani struggles to maintain his faith in the midst of his traumatic experience. He is first arrested while conducting a church service: "I expected God to intervene. After all, was I not preaching the truth? . . . I looked all around me, and finally straight into the overcast sky, but

14. Breyten Breytenbach, *The True Confessions of an Albino Terrorist* (London: Faber & Faber, 1984).

15. Tshenuwani Simon Farisani, *Diary from a South African Prison*, ed. John A. Evenson (Philadelphia: Fortress, 1987), 8.

God seemed to have retired behind those unthinking black clouds."[16]
During his initial three months of detention, Farisani is physically
unharmed but daily hears the screams of other tortured prisoners.
Eventually he, too, is brutalized: dangled headfirst out of a third-floor
window, beaten with sticks and chairs, tortured with electric shocks on
his genitals, repeatedly doused with water. He describes such treatment
with remarkable constraint in simple, matter-of-fact, factual prose.

But Farisani's spiritual distress is rendered in messier terms. If God
exists, how can he allow such things to happen? Prayer after prayer
is unanswered: he asks for manna from heaven to replace his worm-
infested food, for his prison door to open like Paul and Silas's, and
even, after the worst torture, to be allowed to die. "The god of Pretoria
had the upper hand," he concludes at one point. "*My* heavenly Father
was for all intents and purposes dead."[17]

Farisani begins to lose a sense of himself as he is isolated from his
community and becomes merely a hurting, throbbing lump of flesh.
His torturers tell him he is a communist terrorist, but Farisani tries
to maintain his identity as a pastor, a man of God. Yet that religious
identity is challenged by doubt and despair. *Diary from a South African
Prison* alternates between periods of despair and times when Farisani feels God's presence. This presence comes in two ways: mediated
through others and directly from God. Left alone in an exercise area,
Farisani is heartened when other detainees peer out their windows
and urgently whisper, "Umfundisi! Umfundisi!" (Pastor! Pastor!). He
rejoices: "They knew me. They also knew that I am a pastor, a man of
God. Detention or no detention, I was still a man of God, a pastor."[18]
Even greater comfort occurs when "the silence is broken," in the words
of a chapter title, and Farisani has a series of mystical visions.

After three periods of intense physical torture, Farisani "confesses"
in a written account stating what his abusers want to hear—not the
truth, but fabrications about terrorists wielding AK-47s and his church
serving as a front for subversive activity. The *Diary* ultimately becomes
his true confession, for he is full of guilt about these previous lies:
"My Christian brothers and sisters, my God, please forgive me. I could

16. Ibid., 17.
17. Ibid., 50.
18. Ibid., 49.

not take more torture."[19] But when his imprisoners encourage him to commit suicide, he resists, believing that control over his life and death belongs to God: "Better that I should make false confessions, which I could later retract, than take away life which no man can restore."[20]

Farisani does retract his falsehoods and learns how to reclaim his identity by telling his story—first on a world speaking tour sponsored by Amnesty International and then in a documentary film, *The Torture of a South African Pastor* (1983). Consequentially, he was detained for a fourth time in November 1986 and released in January 1987 only after enormous international pressure. While being treated at the Center for Torture Victims in Saint Paul, Minnesota, Farisani wrote *Diary from a South African Prison*. His story was publically rehearsed again when he testified before the Truth and Reconciliation Commission in 1996. Farisani was elected to the Limpopo Provincial Legislature in 1997, where he became Speaker of the House in 2004.

Farisani's story demonstrates his deep faith and attests to his *ubuntu* identity. His book informs readers about the atrocities committed under the South African apartheid regime, as well as the daily details of life in a country of spectacular natural sights and tremendous human poverty. But beyond instruction, his narrative is also emotionally resonant and spiritually challenging; the reader is invited to mourn, to doubt, to forgive, and to believe. While we may rejoice that conditions in South Africa today, although not perfect, are immeasurably improved from the 1970s and 1980s, Farisani's account reminds us that Christians around the world—in China, Turkey, and Pakistan—are still undergoing torture and death, facing the same kind of religious questions and dilemmas chronicled so powerfully in this memoir. Much prayer, mourning, and reform remains to be done. Shalom is still distant.

The Truth and Reconciliation Hearings

My research about and experiences in South Africa revealed how interconnected the different types of confessional modes had become in the 1990s. The life-affirming aspects of religious confession were

19. Ibid., 72.
20. Ibid., 49.

incorporated into the judicial process through the Truth and Reconciliation process, which, in turn, became a major topic of South
African memoirs, poems, and novels. The Truth and Reconciliation
Commission (TRC) had been established in 1995 to facilitate national
reconciliation by creating a public record of human rights violations
under apartheid. Victims testified about their experiences; perpetrators confessed their actions. In essence, a new national narrative was
written through these testimonies and admissions.

From February 1996 through 1997, victims recounted their stories
at hearings held in crowded courtrooms, city halls, and community
centers. Beginning in the fall of 1996, the TRC's Amnesty Committee heard amnesty applications. Faced with the compromises necessary to a negotiated settlement, South Africa decided to establish
the TRC process rather than pursue legal prosecutions of those who
had committed abuses. This was a conscious choice of truth rather
than justice, with the goal of reconciliation, as the Promotion of
National Unity and Reconciliation Act states: "There is a need for
understanding but not for vengeance, a need for reparation but not
for retaliation, a need for ubuntu but not for victimization."[21] While
some observers criticized the abandonment of justice, others argued
for the greater value of the truth that would be spoken as a way of
healing and forming a new South African community.

The Christian roots of the TRC process were unmistakable, beginning with the appointment of Archbishop Desmond Tutu as TRC
chair. At the first meeting of the TRC on December 16, 1995, Tutu
established the narrative framework of the commission's work in
Christian terms: "We will be engaging in what should be a corporate
nationwide process of healing through contrition, confession and
forgiveness."[22] Yet Tutu also acknowledged the need for ecumenical
religious confession to complement the judicial proceedings: "I hope
that our churches, mosques, synagogues and temples will be able to
provide liturgies for corporate confession and absolution."

Some critics, such as Andre De Toit, questioned the imposition of
a Christian paradigm on a secular process: "As religious leaders and

21. See http://www.justice.gov.za/legislation/acts/1995-034.pdf.
22. Information about the TRC, including quotations from the hearings, has been
taken from the official TRC website at www.justice.gov.za.

churches became increasingly involved in the commission's work, the influence of religious style and symbolism supplanted political and human rights concerns."[23] Some victims, such as Marius Schoon, whose entire family was killed by the South African Security Forces, objected to the TRC's "imposition of a Christian morality of forgiveness."[24] There is no question that the TRC proceedings involved religious symbolism and language, but, in the case of the victims' testimony, much of that arose spontaneously out of an unfathomable sustaining personal faith, and the Christian morality of forgiveness was not required by the process.

In the summer of 1996, I attended a TRC hearing in Pietermaritzburg, Natal, held in a baroque brick city hall. Television spotlights flooded an elevated platform that held three rectangular tables covered in white linen and two crude wooden booths for translators who provided simultaneous translations in Zulu and English. The TRC commissioners slowly assembled on the stage before the proceedings were opened with a Zulu prayer offered by a Methodist commissioner. Then Dumisa Ntsebeza, chair of the day's hearings, solemnly lit a white candle symbolizing the presence of truth, much like the Christ candle used in Christian church services. Next, the audience was asked to stand, and the victims slowly filed into the front rows of the hall. In typical legal proceedings, the audience rises for the judge, but at the TRC hearings, the highest honor was given to the victims. The commissioners came down from the platform to welcome the victims personally—shaking hands, embracing, kissing. Many of the victims were already sobbing, overcome by the fact that an official government representative was showing them respect.

As each victim went up to testify, family members gathered around, and a psychotherapist provided additional support. Before the testimony began, one commissioner asked about the victim's family—parents, spouse, children, siblings—their names, ages, where they lived, how they were employed. Besides putting the witness at ease, this ritual grounded him or her as a person in the fullest African sense—with a family, a

23. Martha Minow, *Between Vengeance and Forgiveness: Facing History after Genocide and Mass Violence* (Boston: Beacon Press, 1998), 55.

24. Timothy Garton Ash, "True Confessions," *The New York Review*, July 17, 1997.

community, a place. Then devastating stories were recounted: intimidations, assaults, abductions, rapes, torture, and murder. A woman in her early forties recounted the assassination of her husband, an African Congress community leader who was shot on the beautiful road winding through the valleys between Pietermaritzburg and Ixhopo, the town that Alan Paton describes so lyrically in *Cry, the Beloved Country*. She was left with five young children. "I wanted to kill all my children and myself," she said. "Sometimes, I still do." With one exception, the victims I heard during two days of hearings all spoke of their experiences in Christian language, as part of a Christian narrative. Biblical texts, impassioned prayers, and God's miraculous interventions were reported. "When I think of the things that have happened," one dignified matron said, "I just open the Bible and pray Psalm 71."

At each testimony's conclusion, the commissioners asked what kind of reparation the victim requested. The requests were minimal: one woman wanted a plaque put up on the site of her husband's murder; a young man, confined to a wheelchair because of a bullet in his spine, asked for financial aid to attend college; a weeping mother said, "I have no particular request, I just wish to know who killed my son." Finally, a commissioner gave a formal response that summarized the testimony, affirmed the victim, and declared the wrongs that had been committed. "We have a system that needs overhauling, a system that needs to re-earn your trust," one said; "testimony such as yours will assist in the process of creating a just system." The profound respect, serious listening, and sense of safety instilled by these rituals were all designed to "reestablish . . . a moral framework, in which wrongs are correctly named and condemned," as Martha Minow describes.[25]

For some South Africans, the confessional discourse of the perpetrators was the most disturbing aspect of the TRC process. The extent of the former state's involvement in human rights abuses, with poisoned clothing, booby-trapped Walkmans, roaming murder squads, and dismembered corpses, stunned many white South Africans, and the often-graphic details made amnesty difficult to accept. The perpetrators' confessions were not coerced, although the prospect of amnesty served as strong motivation. Nonetheless, the decision to testify was

---

25. Minow, *Between Vengeance*, 71.

a gamble, for if amnesty were not granted, the testimony could be used in later legal proceedings. Amnesty was contingent on a full confession and demonstration that violations of human rights were committed in pursuit of political objectives. However, the perpetrators' statements did not have to indicate remorse or ask for forgiveness, and the failure of some individuals to demonstrate sorrow for their actions was frustrating for many observers.

Some perpetrators issued apparently genuine requests for forgiveness, but others were struck with the futility of such contrition. One member of the notorious Vlakplaas Five death squad told a journalist, "You know, you say you're sorry, but on the other hand, it is also empty words. . . . Do you understand what I am trying to say? I mean here I walk up to a person I don't even know . . . and I say, 'listen here, I'm sorry,' I mean isn't it just empty words?"[26] In a reversal of the victims' testimony, perpetrators' statements were required to be constative speech acts—conveying information—but not illocutionary acts of contrition or penitence. And even as perpetrators were not required to express contrition in order to receive amnesty, neither were victims required to forgive their wrongdoers. In these two important ways, the TRC's judicial confession differed from Christian confession.

Although Bishop Tutu's infectious advocacy of Christian forgiveness and some victims' passionate faith inspired them to embrace those who had wronged them in transcendental acts of forgiveness, others found themselves unable to forgive, and the legal process did not require it. Christian confession thus made three major contributions to the TRC process: it provided a moral standard of good and evil, a set of images and rhetoric in which the process could be conducted, and a declaration of the centrality of community for personal identity.

As a thoroughly public process, saturating the radio, television, and print media, the TRC hearings constructed a new national narrative for an emerging country, with a collection of images, characters, plots, motifs, and—most crucially—values. The hearings were open to the public, an official website was frequently updated, and proceedings were constantly discussed in public forums, newspaper commentaries, and academic conferences. Although some South Africans grew

26. Krog, *Country of My Skull*, 117.

tired of the widespread preoccupation with the TRC (writer Rian
Malan complained about having to mix "breakfast and blood" in
the mornings), the hearings gripped the South African imagination.

In analyzing the public discourse associated with the TRC process
as a narrative text, I took my definition of literature's assorted forms
and functions, its ways of acting in and impacting the world, to perhaps its most extreme lengths. However, the TRC's public drama of
confession was followed by many confessional texts in more traditional
literary genres. What fiction writer Njabulo Ndebele calls "the restoration of narrative," initiated by the TRC, continues in post-apartheid
literature, with many writers believing, along with Andre Brink, that
"unless the enquiries of the Truth and Reconciliation Commission
(TRC) are extended, complicated, and intensified in the imaginings
of literature, society cannot sufficiently come to terms with its past
to face the future."[27] The TRC process inspired a flood of fiction,
drama, and memoir, such as *A Duty of Memory* (1997), *Ubu and
Truth Commission* (1998), and *Country of My Skull* (1998), all of
which can be interpreted in the light of the confessional mode.

I spent the 1995–96 academic year working on the theoretical and
historical chapters of *Truth and Reconciliation*, followed by the summer of 1996 in South Africa where, in addition to working in libraries
and archives, I heard stunning performances of orature (including a
praise poem delivered to Nelson Mandela), talked with poet Mazisi
Kunene (translator of *Shaka the Great*), attended South African theater productions, and witnessed two TRC hearings. But in the fall
of 1996, I returned to full-time teaching, and it took six more years
before *Truth and Reconciliation* was issued as part of the Heinemann
Studies in African Literature series. My teaching responsibilities gave
me less time for writing, but the difficulties of academic publishing,
including some distinctive problems associated with writing about
African literature, also played a role in the amount of time it took
for the book to appear.

27. Njabulo S. Ndebele, "Memory, Metaphor, and the Triumph of Narrative,"
in *Negotiating the Past: The Making of Memory in South Africa*, ed. Sarah Nuttall
and Carli Coetzee (Cape Town: Oxford University Press, 1998), 27; Andre Brink,
"Stories of History: Reimagining the Past in Post-Apartheid Narrative," in Nuttall
and Coetzee, *Negotiating the Past*, 30.

Fair Use and Writing about African Literature

Heinemann had been my first choice for a publisher, as it was the leading trade publisher in African literature, with a long history of publishing works by and about African writers. It also distributed its books in Africa, unlike most American academic or trade presses. The Heinemann African Writers Series (AWS) originated in 1962 as a source of inexpensive textbooks for newly independent African countries moving from an exclusive focus on European literature to teach works from their own country and area. The AWS published major contemporary African writers, along with earlier works, orature transcriptions, traditional folk material, and nonfiction accounts of African culture and history. With an extensive distribution system in the United States, Britain, and Commonwealth nations, Heinemann also played a pivotal role in introducing Western readers to African literature through both the AWS and the scholarly books published in the Studies in African Literature (SAL) series, which initially were also available in cheap paperback editions.[28] But in 2000, after Heinemann had accepted my book proposal, Greenwood took over the SAL series. So while *Truth and Reconciliation* was still technically in the Heinemann series, the book's editing, publishing, and publicity were handled by Greenwood, which issued it in an expensive hardcover edition, well out of the price range of most African readers, much to my dismay. In the world of trade publications, shifting ownership, takeovers, and buyouts can significantly affect an academic author.[29]

Although I submitted my complete manuscript in March 2001, Greenwood did not start editing or typesetting for a full year, until I had obtained the necessary permissions to reprint material, a key element of any literary study. In the United States, in order to include any previously published material beyond that deemed in "fair use," one must obtain the permission of the copyright holder. The ambiguous legal definition of "fair use" prompts publishers to exercise

---

28. For an inside account of Heinemann's formation of the African literary canon, see James Currey, *Africa Writes Back: The African Writers Series and the Launch of African Literature* (Athens: Ohio University Press, 2008).

29. More recently, Greenwood Publications has been acquired by Houghton Mifflin Harcourt.

extreme, often unreasonable, caution in what they will allow to be quoted. At this point in my professional career, I had published four academic books, each with a different publisher, each of whom had had a slightly different interpretation of "fair use." The total words quoted that required permissions differed; the definition of making a reasonable attempt to find the permission holder differed; and the way of counting the words differed. According to Greenwood's house rules, quoting more than one line of poetry and more than three hundred words of prose required permission, which needed to be obtained in writing from all copyright holders and needed to cover all editions in all languages. One might think that authors would be pleased with scholarly discussions that facilitate their entry into the pedagogical and academic canon, but some writers make obtaining permissions difficult if not impossible. Identifying, locating, contacting, and hearing back from the copyright holders of African texts adds a level of complication to scholarship on African literature that the Shakespearean scholar, for example, doesn't face.

The manuscript of *Truth and Reconciliation* included extensive textual analyses of ten South African writers. As a Bakhtinian critic, I believe in allowing the multiple voices of a text and author to speak along with my own assessment and analysis. Furthermore, evidence of "confessional" aspects is often revealed through diction and rhetoric. Hence, the manuscript was brimming with quotations. Locating the copyright holders and requesting the world rights for more than ten South African works, with multiple editions published in South Africa, Great Britain, France, the Netherlands, and the United States in different years, proved difficult.

Noni Jabavu, for example, posed extraordinary problems. She was a remarkable writer—one of the first black South African women to publish internationally, but a controversial figure who had largely been ignored by the critics. A well-educated, middle-class South African, Jabavu went to England for schooling in 1933, married an Englishman, and did not return to South Africa until 1955, after the establishment of apartheid. Her memoir, *The Ochre People*, was first published in England in 1964. Jabavu eventually moved to Zimbabwe, and in 1982 *The Ochre People* was republished in South Africa by Ravan Press, a noted anti-apartheid publisher. Jabavu wrote an introduction for this edition expressing her admiration for the anti-apartheid movement. The Ravan edition, which I purchased in South Africa in 1996, indicated that the copyright had been reissued to Jabavu in 1982. However, I had no idea if or where she was living, and an extensive internet search did not turn up any information about Ravan.

When I emailed the head of African Literature at the University of the Witwatersrand to ask for help, Dr. James Ogude promptly replied that he could not find an email address for Ravan, had "heard rumours that they may have folded up," but had found a street address and fax number, which he kindly emailed me. I immediately sent off both an airmail letter and a fax, but the fax number was no longer operational, and I received no reply to my letter. In September I discovered that Ohio University Press was distributing some of Ravan's publications in the United States, so I contacted them; a month later they informed me that Macmillan Press, in Great Britain, had taken over Ravan.

By the end of October, I finally heard from Macmillan only to learn that in 1996 Jabavu had instructed Ravan not to grant any permissions for *The Ochre People*. The Macmillan staff did not know whether she was still alive or not, but they would look into it. With no word by December and Greenwood still insisting on a written permission, my only option was to eliminate enough quotations from *The Ochre People* to bring citations below three hundred words. The paraphrases I used instead considerably muted Jabavu's affecting, elegant voice. Similar difficulties contacting copyright holders occurred with at least half of the authors I was discussing in *Truth and Reconciliation*, although I was able to track down almost all of them eventually.

Quotations from another text were cut for a different reason. Living authors often either hold their own copyright or instruct their publisher not to issue permission to quote until they have reviewed the request personally. Living authors thus can essentially censor or at least muffle those scholars who are critical of them. In my discussion of a memoir called *My Traitor's Heart* by Rian Malan, I criticized Malan's bad faith and self-righteous justification, as well as identified his racist rhetoric and subtexts. I was convinced that Malan wasn't going to like what I had to say, so I didn't even try to get permission to cite him. Instead I converted most of my quotations to paraphrases and summaries. This did not stop my criticism, but it did dull it by making me unable to allow Malan to damn himself with his own words. And since a great deal of my point had to do with the language that he chose, this weakened my argument. But despite the demands of detective work, exasperating delays, and unwelcome editing, *Truth and Reconciliation* at last was published in 2002.[30] By that point, I felt as if I had been wrestling with my own white whale for many years.

30. I discussed writing about South African literature in the context of American publication law for a session held at the Modern Language Association in 2003 sponsored by the Society for Critical Exchange. The full account can be read at http://www.cwru.edu/affil/sce/MLA_2003.htm.

❖ 5 ❖

The Monkey-Rope

2000–

After the marathon of *Truth and Reconciliation*, professional and personal exigencies kept me from concentrated work in African literature for ten years. Professionally, I moved into faculty development work. As Lavinia Dickinson said about her sister Emily's withdrawal from social life, "It was only a happen," a gradual process with no instigating moment of decision, guided by more mysterious providential currents.

Following the publication of *Literature Through the Eyes of Faith*, I had been invited to present several lectures and workshops on teaching with gender sensitivity, expanding the canon, and multicultural education. In the late 1990s, I joined Arthur Holmes, Harold Heie, and Stan Gaede as a facilitator for the annual summer national CCCU New Faculty Workshop, and I began to speak occasionally about faculty development at Christian colleges and universities. Simultaneously, I was invited to join the Pew Preparing Future Faculty (PFF) project, a national program with the goal of reforming American graduate education by preparing graduate students to be teachers and informing them about work life at community colleges, private liberal arts institutions, and comprehensive universities. With other local faculty from non-research institutions, I became part of the PFF program at the University of Washington, helping UW graduate students to understand the role of a faculty member at a mission-driven, teaching institution. When the founding director of the SPU New Faculty Seminar stepped down, I also picked up that responsibility.

A brief intellectual hiatus began in 2000, when I was diagnosed with breast cancer and went through fifteen months of treatment and resulting chemo-brain and exhaustion. Excellent medical care and the prayers of many led to a full recovery, and in 2002 I was appointed director of the newly founded SPU Center for Scholarship and Faculty Development (CSFD), in conjunction with serving as the codirector for SPU's SERVE (Spiritual and Educational Resources for Vocational Exploration) program, sponsored by the Lilly Foundation's Program for the Theological Exploration of Vocation (PTEV). In these roles, I assisted new faculty in exploring the vocation of a teacher-scholar, managed faculty scholarship and mentoring programs, conducted pedagogical consultations and workshops, and supervised faculty grant writing. I continued to teach one or two courses a year to keep my pedagogical skills honed, but the English department hired someone else to teach African literature—Kimberly Wedeven Segall, who did graduate work in South African literature at Northwestern University after her undergraduate years at Calvin, where she had studied with me. To my delight, the next generation was now teaching African literature.

Forming Faithful Faculty: Head and Heart

My faculty development work was grounded in Reformed educational philosophy. The PFF program had confirmed my own experience that graduate education did little to prepare future faculty to be teachers, to work at small undergraduate institutions, to participate in a learning community's life and worship, or to contribute to a religiously informed educational mission. Many faculty had never faced the challenge or had the opportunity to think through the ways in which their deepest beliefs affected, informed, or conflicted with their disciplinary practices, pedagogical choices, or research agendas. Graduate school professionalized budding faculty in highly limited ways, preparing them for positions at secular research institutions and mandating either overtly or implicitly that issues of Christian faith were private with no application or meaning for the academic life. Christian colleges often endorsed the integration of faith and learning, but new faculty—especially those with no personal experience of Christian education—needed resources and support to discern how their faith might inform their teaching and scholarship.

Therefore, I stressed basic philosophical and theological work, such as identifying the foundational premises of one's discipline, field, or theoretical school and then comparing those assumptions with one's Christian beliefs. I also encouraged faculty to consider their views on the *telos* of education, the nature of students as human beings, the unspoken assumptions behind established curricula, and the role of moral or ethical judgments in their discipline. In SPU's New Faculty Workshop, first-year faculty had the opportunity to read about these issues and to explore and develop their own thoughts in writing, discussions, and storytelling sessions.

However, the ecumenical nature of SPU faculty—which included those from Roman Catholic, Greek Orthodox, Lutheran, Presbyterian, Mennonite, Methodist, Baptist, Assemblies of God, and nondenominational Bible churches—resulted in a variety of configurations of faith and learning, with much more theological diversity than found at Calvin. Seattle Pacific University embraces a community faith identity that is historically orthodox, clearly evangelical, genuinely ecumenical, and informed by the Wesleyan tradition, and job applicants write an essay about how their own faith tradition and practice fits within this context.

Before coming to SPU, I had developed some wariness about evangelical and Wesleyan attitudes toward the intellect. At Westmont and in my work with the CCCU, I had discovered the theological illiteracy of many evangelicals, who lacked the blessings of catechetical instruction. For evangelicals and Wesleyans, heart often appeared to trump head, which, in an institution dedicated to education, seemed misguided. Few scholarly discussions of faith and learning from a

Wesleyan perspective even existed. Mark Noll's indictment of the scandal of the evangelical mind, which identified the Wesleyan holiness tradition's "stress on the dangers of the world" and "the comforts of separated piety" as significant contributing factors to the dearth of Christian scholarship,[1] was uncomfortably reminiscent of aspects of my childhood. The identity of many evangelical colleges was determined more by expressions and structures of overt piety—such as strict lifestyle requirements, mandatory chapel attendance, and *de rigueur* opening prayers in classes—than by intellectual concepts, philosophical moorings, and ways of thought.

But a few years at SPU taught me much about the role of spiritual development in Christian education, about the need to involve the heart as well as the mind in one's teaching and scholarship, and about the value of the spiritual disciplines, the liturgy, and the sacraments. Randy L. Maddox, the Paul T. Walls Professor of Wesleyan Theology, was instrumental in introducing me to the Wesley I never knew. Despite the strong pietistic and legalistic strain in American Methodism, Wesley himself was a well-read eighteenth-century scholar who advocated "plundering the Egyptians" for intellectual gold. He stressed lay education, produced a fifty-volume *Christian Library* that included Eastern Orthodox, Roman Catholic, German Pietist, and Reformed authors, and designed extensive reading programs in literature and science. What eventually became known as the Wesleyan quadrilateral (although Wesley never used that term) emphasized an epistemology that drew on Scripture, tradition, reason, and experience—not simply experience and Scripture. Wesley was far more of a head person than I had given him credit for being.

Yet his Aldersgate experience—feeling his heart touched by God years after his head endorsed Christianity—caused Wesley to resolve, "[Let us] unite the pair so long disjoined, / Knowledge and vital Piety."[2] In one sermon he warned, "We know that wrong opinions in religion

1. Mark Noll, *The Scandal of the Evangelical Mind* (Grand Rapids: Eerdmans, 1994), 120.
2. Charles Wesley, "Hymn 461, for Children," in *The Works of John Wesley*, vol. 7, *A Collection of Hymns for the Use of the People Called Methodists*, ed. Franz Hildebrandt and Oliver A. Beckerlegge (New York: Oxford University Press, 1983; repr., Nashville: Abingdon, 1989), 643–44.

naturally lead to wrong tempers, or wrong practices; and that it is our bonded duty to pray that we might have a right judgment in all things. But still a man may judge as accurately as the devil, and yet be as wicked as he."[3] Right knowing, while crucial, did not necessarily carry over into right living or loving. Salvation, Wesley held, involved more than simply forgiveness of sins. His favorite metaphor for God was Doctor, one who worked through the Spirit to heal our warped lives spiritually, emotionally, and physically. Although as a Calvinist I remained skeptical of Wesley's belief that complete sanctification on this present earth was possible, and although I was convinced that the deep scars of original sin were well confirmed by history, Wesley's unwavering affirmation of God's transforming power to heal was inspiring. Combining the Reformed responsibility to think carefully and work toward shalom with the Wesleyan idea of spiritual growth and service to others brought head and heart together in new ways for me.

While the Reformed tradition stressed the importance of identifying presuppositions and foundational beliefs in one's worldview, Wesley was concerned with the ways in which a Christian worldview could be methodically developed through practices as well as ideas. I had previously struggled with some of the apparent contradictions in many discussions of worldview, which was associated with propositional truths, theological foundations, and philosophical categories (ontology, epistemology, etc.) but was also defined as prescientific or pretheoretical, a basic human tendency across cultures and generations. However, if worldviews are unreflective expressions of basic beliefs, why would we try to identify and teach students about a Christian worldview? If students were Christians, wouldn't they already have a Christian worldview? How could we explain the human ability to hold inconsistent beliefs and to operate with assumptions at odds with Christian faith? Charts outlining categorical differences between the Christian worldview and other worldviews (deism, naturalism, nihilism, existentialism, or postmodernism) implied that a Christian worldview would be molded if one had the right philosophy.[4]

3. *John Wesley's Sermons: An Anthology*, ed. Albert C. Outler and Richard Heitzenrater (Nashville: Abingdon, 1991), 563.
4. For example, James W. Sire, *The Universe Next Door: A Basic Worldview Catalog*, 4th ed. (Downers Grove, IL: InterVarsity, 2004).

As Jonathan Edwards notes, however, the formation of the will also plays a crucial role in Christian identity.

Like Edwards, Wesley believed that a Christian worldview was the product not only of the head but also of the heart; believers' temperaments and practices, as well as their ways of thought, are formed by nurturing and shaping. Thus, Wesley did not write systematic theologies or apologetics but rather crafted liturgies, hymns, sermons, prayer books, spiritual biographies, devotional practices, and spiritual exercises.

Wesley's thought complements an emerging strand in Reformed thinking that emphasizes the narrative rather than the propositional status of worldviews.[5] As narratives, worldviews recount a story of identity and purpose, including paradoxes and inconsistencies. A person's or community's narrative is constantly unfurling in dialogical interaction with life experiences, traditions, historical processes, and contextual realities, so that I choose what I believe, esteem, and practice even as my upbringing, social position, and cultural milieu also form predispositions in me. Worldview and life experiences ebb and flow in impact as I live out and compose my story within the larger narrative of God's work in the world. Narrative worldview thinking led me to newly appreciate the value of service learning, travel abroad, multicultural experiences, spiritual disciplines, and liturgical routines within a Christian education, and to include these issues in SPU's faculty development programs.

Globalization and Literary Study

As director of the CSFD, I primarily researched and wrote about faculty development,[6] but as a secondary interest, I also began to write about the study of African literature in light of globalization and the growth of world Christianity.[7] Globalization had become a common

5. See my *Joining the Mission: A Guide for (Mainly) New College Faculty* (Grand Rapids: Eerdmans, 2011), 116–21.

6. The culmination of this work is *Joining the Mission*.

7. See my "Imagining Globalization as a Christian Literary Critic," in *The Gospel and Globalization: Exploring the Religious Roots of a Globalized World*, ed. Michael W. Goheen and Erin G. Glanville (Vancouver, BC: Regent College Publishing,

way of defining and understanding the world in both the academy and the media by the turn of the century. In 2002, a special issue of *PMLA* called "Globalizing Literary Studies" highlighted these changes: "The challenge for students of the humanities . . . is not to decide whether globalization deserves to be taken seriously but how best to engage it critically."[8] Simultaneously, historians were chronicling the demographic turn south in world Christianity, but few literary critics had noticed this conjunction or commented on its implications. So I began to argue that, on the one hand, Christian literary scholars should study and address the impact of globalization, and, on the other hand, secular literary scholars should recognize and consider the impact of world Christianity on literature. A monkey-rope connects us all.

Melville's account of the monkey-rope highlights one of the most appealing features of *Moby-Dick*: Ishmael's unconventional friendship with a tattooed South Seas islander named Queequeg. The two meet in New Bedford when the landlord of the Spouter-Inn, perhaps as a joke, gives them a room together. Initially, Ishmael is repulsed by what he assumes to be a barbaric cannibal, but he then considers the situation more calmly: "I stood looking at him a moment. For all his tattooings he was on the whole a clean, comely looking cannibal. What's all this fuss I have been making about, thought I to myself—the man's a human being just as I am: he has just as much reason to fear me, as I have to be afraid of him. Better sleep with a sober cannibal than a drunken Christian."[9] The unlikely duo become bosom companions, shipping aboard the *Pequod* together to chase the white whale. Ishmael's ability to recognize and embrace Queequeg's humanity is a crucial part of a narrative in which another character, Captain Ahab, is so obsessed with his desire for revenge that he turns everyone else on board into mere tools, pieces of machinery to serve his crazed purpose.

Queequeg is a skilled harpooner, and Ishmael assists as his bowman, so when a whale is killed and the carcass tethered alongside the

---

2009), 323–40; and "Reading and Faith in a Global Community," *Christianity and Literature* 54 (2005): 323–40.

8. Giles Gunn, "Introduction: Globalizing Literary Studies," *PMLA* 116 (2001): 21. Other theme issues on globalization in literary studies include *Cultural Critique* (2004), *American Literature* (2006), and *Modern Language Quarterly* (2007).

9. Melville, *Moby-Dick*, 51.

ship, they must work together on a grim task. Queequeg is lowered onto the back of the dead mammal to guide the blubber hook as it strips the whale of its valuable commodity, and for safety purposes, Ishmael belays him "by what is technically called in the fishery a monkey-rope, attached to a strong strip of canvas belted round his waist." The monkey-rope creates a strange union that epitomizes their friendship:

> It was a humorously perilous business for both of us. For . . . the monkey-rope was fast at both ends; fast to Queequeg's broad canvas belt, and fast to my narrow leather one. So that for better or for worse, we two, for the time, were wedded; and should poor Queequeg sink to rise no more, then both usage and honor demanded, that instead of cutting the cord, it should drag me down in his wake. So, then, an elongated Siamese ligature united us. Queequeg was my own inseparable twin brother; nor could I any way get rid of the dangerous liabilities which the hempen bond entailed.[10]

The philosophical Ishmael soon realizes the symbolism of their condition: "I saw that this situation of ours was the precise situation of every mortal that breathes; only, in most cases, he, one way or other, has this Siamese connexion [sic] with a plurality of other mortals. If your banker breaks, you snap; if your apothecary by mistake sends you poison in your pills, you die."[11] Humanity is inexorably linked in a vast chain of relationships that brings together cannibal and Christian, harpooner and bowman, grand captain and common sailor. Given such interdependence, we should practice what Ishmael calls "the very milk and sperm of kindness."[12]

Moby-Dick, often considered the quintessential American novel, is also an exemplary global novel about the multiple monkey-ropes of life. The microcosmic Pequod sails the seas with a motley crew made up of every tribe and nation. Furthermore, in the novel's cetological chapters, Ishmael scours literature, philosophy, religion, art, history, and science in an attempt to understand the whale, discovering connections everywhere, a vast web of ideas and images in which one

10. Ibid., 414–16.
11. Ibid., 416.
12. Ibid., 533.

thing can always lead to something else, in which an individual is always part of a larger community, in which manifold monkey-ropes encircle and unite us all. More than a century before the theory entered the academy, Melville was describing the course and consequences of globalization.

The term *globalization* refers to the fact that the world is becoming a "shared social space," so that what happens in one part of the world has substantial consequences for people in another part of the world: "Globalization [is] the widening, deepening and speeding up of worldwide interconnectedness in all aspects of contemporary social life, from the cultural to the criminal, the financial to the spiritual."[13] Globalization involves connections across the planet, connections created and analyzed in a variety of ways but frequently described with the metaphor of "flow." For example, one definition states that globalization involves complex patterns of "economic, military, technological, ecological, migratory, political and cultural flows."[14]

While social scientists study economic and political currents, literary critics analyze the textual and symbolic streams, for, as Giles Gunn declares, "Cultural interactions, negotiations, and transformations have often proved at least as fateful as economic or political ones if only because the former have frequently determined the way the latter could be understood and actualized."[15] Because the metaphors, symbols, narratives, and interpretations found in texts have social and personal formative power, literary texts are principal elements of globalization, and the study of literature in the twenty-first century has increasingly been conducted in this light. One key finding has been the degree to which different cultures are entangled with each other: "Cultural interpenetration and intermingling have become the global norm."[16] Even the Western intellectual tradition is less pristine

13. David Held, Anthony McGrew, David Goldblatt, and Jonathan Perraton, · *Global Transformations: Politics, Economics, and Culture* (Stanford: Stanford University Press, 1999), 1, 2.

14. Ibid., 7. Some globalization theory acknowledges that global eddies and flows across the globe have always existed. As a geographer friend says, "The internet is the modern version of Paul's Roman roads."

15. Gunn, "Introduction: Globalizing Literary Studies," 21.

16. Frederick Buell, *National Culture and the New Global System* (Baltimore: Johns Hopkins University Press, 1994), 312.

than we previously thought. Technological advances have facilitated such mashups, for better and worse; social media's constructive role in advancing democracy in the Arab Spring, for example, is accompanied by its destructive role in instigating violence through one inflammatory anti-Muslim video or cartoon. Globalization also informs literary settings, plots, and themes, such as world cities, conflicting global identities, and anti-globalization protests. Technology and globalization also have important consequences for the production, reception, and circulation of literary texts. With international publishing conglomerates, the information superhighway, and ubiquitous air transportation, many writers, such as Salman Rushdie, Haruki Murakami, Zadie Smith, and Gao Xingjian, are identified as global authors rather than by national or even linguistic labels.

However, one major tide often overlooked in discussions about the globalization of literary studies is the worldwide growth of Christianity. As economics, politics, and cultures have become increasingly global, so, too, has Christianity. Modernization and postcolonialism have led not to secularization, as was once expected, but rather to an unprecedented expansion of and major demographic shift in religious faith.

For example, the once widespread assumption that Christianity would dwindle and die in Africa as colonial powers withdrew and independence was achieved has been decisively proven incorrect. Instead, whether during postcolonial democratic independence, an ensuing socialist state, or a dictatorial regime, Christianity continued to grow in Africa. In fact, more Africans have converted to Christianity since the end of colonial rule than in the entire period of colonialism, and by the year 2025, it is projected that Africa will have more than 600 million Christians, the largest single bloc of Christians in the world.[17] As Christianity increasingly becomes a non-Western religion, the literature from global population centers will be produced in Christian societies. Missiologist Andrew Walls predicts that the massive relocations of Christianity in the twenty-first century will produce a cultural transformation like that which took place in the early Chris-

17. David B. Barrett, George Thomas Kurian, and Todd M. Johnson, eds., *World Christian Encyclopedia: A Comparative Survey of Churches and Religions in the Modern World* (Oxford: Oxford University Press, 2001).

tian church's encounter with Greek culture. If, as Gunn says, symbolic interactions, negotiations, and transformations determine the way in which economic and political interactions are understood and actualized, they play an even more significant role in religious interactions. Both literature and Christianity will undergo change as Christian beliefs are transmitted, received, and expressed in different cultures, customs, and traditions. Rather than a unidirectional current of Western Christianity flooding Africa, there is a complex multidirectional ebb and flow, an endlessly dancing monkey-rope.

Consequently, I began to argue—beginning at a national MLA Convention session on teaching world literature in 2007—that one of the most significant but little noted contexts for teaching contemporary world literature from the global South, in general, and from Africa, in particular, was the explosive growth of Christianity.[18] We need to understand this phenomenon to avoid misreading or overlooking significant elements of the literature from the global South, for Christianity plays an integral part in contemporary African life. Deborah Klein, who taught for eight years at the Federal University of Jos, Nigeria, attests, "In truth, more and more these days Christianity is part of the warp and woof of most African life. . . . Whether hostile or friendly, very few African writers (except perhaps those in exclusively Muslim nations) can ignore the importance of church going in today's Africa."[19] The secular lens of contemporary Western thought may blur and even distort elements of African texts. If we want to move beyond Western-centric analyses to conduct more complex conversations about both our own as well as others' ways of being in the world, we need to take into account what religious historians and demographers call "global Christianity."[20]

Continuing in my early decision to speak not only to the general academy but also to Christian scholars, I advocated for the study of African and global literature in plenary addresses for the Conference

18. A version of this talk later appeared as "African Literature and New Christianity," *Journal of African Children's and Youth Literature* 17–18 (2007–9): 90–93.

19. Deborah Klein, "The Bible as Literature Discussion," online posting to the Christianity and Literature Discussion Group (ChristLit), December 6, 2007.

20. "Global Christianity: A Report on the Size and Distribution of the World's Christian Population," The Pew Forum on Religion and Public Life, December 19, 2011, http://www.pewforum.org/Christian/Global-Christianity-exec.aspx.

on Christianity and Literature and the North American Christian
Foreign Language Association, in talks at Christian colleges and
universities, and in Christian academic journals. In 2012, I edited a
theme issue on "African Narrative and the Christian Tradition" for
Christianity and Literature, highlighting the ways African authors
from across the continent, both Christians and nonbelievers, have
turned (or returned) to the Christian tradition for a toolbox of stories,
characters, and images; for theological concepts of history, leadership,
justice, and solidarity; and for inspiration to practice the ancient art
of crafting identity and meaning through narrative.

While I've added a few drops of water to the rising tide of scholarship in African literature, much work remains to be done in the
expanding field of world literature. Globalization's cultural flows
involve complex interactions between Christianity and literature that
offer prime opportunities for emerging Christian teacher-scholars.
The literary curriculum at Christian colleges and universities needs
to adapt to these global changes. For those of us who study literature
in its assorted relationships with Christianity, globalization provides
new prospects as well as poses crucial questions for future work.

Christian Cosmopolitanism

When I left faculty development to return to full-time teaching in 2010,
I began to think about my work in terms of Christian cosmopolitanism.[21] In intellectual history, the term *cosmopolitanism* arose with the
fourth-century BC philosopher Diogenes the Cynic. When Diogenes
was asked where he came from, he replied, "I am a *kosmopolitēs*,"
which means "a citizen of the world." Diogenes lived at a time when
allegiance to the *polis*, or city-state such as Athens or Sparta, was the
defining characteristic of a Greek free man's identity, so his embrace
of world-citizenship was radical. Extreme political cosmopolitanism advocates for a worldwide government, but moderate political
versions endorse the beneficial ways that states can work together,

21. The following discussion is adapted from my "Christian Cosmopolitanism:
Reading in a Global Age," *Comment*, June 13, 2011, http://www.cardus.ca/comment
/article/2826/christian-cosmopolitanism-reading-in-the-global-age/.

as in the United Nations. Cosmopolitanism also can be understood culturally in practices such as listening to world music, eating ethnic cuisine, and appreciating foreign art forms. The monkey-rope of culture and nation complicates cosmopolitanism. Some fear that as the world becomes more flat, in Thomas Friedman's famous phrase, a tsunami of American television, Coca-Cola, and Hollywood movies will swamp ethnic and national cultures. Perhaps recent instances of violent nationalism are surges against such a threat, for balancing a regard for minority cultures, national identity, and cosmopolitanism is extremely challenging.

At the heart of political and cultural cosmopolitanism lies moral cosmopolitanism, the obligation that human beings take care of each other because they share a common human bond. Doctors without Borders, Amnesty International, and Greenpeace are founded on such a premise. A fundamental element of cosmopolitanism, then, is how one defines those common elements of human identity. For the Greek Stoics, that bond lay in "human argument and aspiration"—that is, the ability to reason and the ability to hope or dream. Enlightenment philosophers used a similar definition to discuss universal human rights.

But Christian cosmopolitanism is premised on the belief that all human beings share an identity as special creations of God, formed in and serving as God's image, designated as daughters and sons of God. The Christian universal community is not based on ethnic identity, skin color, gender, rationality, literacy, social status, or even religious affiliation—all of which have been used at different points in history to draw the boundaries of what it means to be a human being. For Christians, being a human being entails living in the physical creation and dwelling in relationships. We are not *isolatos*, to use a word from *Moby-Dick*, but communal creatures whose identity is premised on relationship both with God and with other human beings.

One articulate defender of moral and cultural cosmopolitanism is Martha Nussbaum, professor of law and ethics at the University of Chicago, who is a strong advocate for "imaginative empathy," believing that the novel engages our sympathy in contemplating lives different from our own and so expands our imaginative capabilities. Reading helps us to develop a moral imagination, and reading, Nussbaum contends, also can help us become more cosmopolitan.

Nussbaum sees the value of reading texts from a variety of cultures in both pragmatic and ethical terms. Pragmatically, reading across cultures provides valuable self-knowledge, as we see ourselves and our customs more clearly by means of contrast, and reading also helps us guard against narrow partisanship. But globalizing our reading also allows us to see others not as opponents, aliens, or inferiors, but instead as fellow human beings, recognizing people's "aspirations to justice and goodness and their capacities for reasoning."[22] Nussbaum argues that we should not give up local allegiances and identities, but rather think of ourselves as surrounded by a series of concentric circles: self, family, neighbors, city, country, and world.

Nussbaum's liberal humanist position is compelling, but her starting point of the individual self gives me pause. Furthermore, like the Stoics, Nussbaum assumes that humans share aspirations to justice and goodness, which I think is an overly optimistic view of human nature. The high premium she puts on universal reason has resulted historically in denying certain people human status on the alleged grounds of their inability to reason; they may be *homo* but they are not *sapiens*. Finally, Nussbaum still prioritizes local identity: "making all human beings like our fellow city dwellers,"[23] rather than seeing those around us as part of a global network of humanity.

Instead of starting with the self at the center, Christian cosmopolitanism begins with the cosmos that includes both the human world and the natural world. This cosmos, according to creation theology, was formed and evolves through God's will. Rather than thinking of ourselves initially as free individual selves; as national citizens with political, economic, or moral obligations; or even as ethically responsible citizens of the world, we should begin with the assumption that we are a part of God's created cosmos.

Furthermore, within this cosmos, human identity and social groupings are more fluid than Nussbaum's concentric circles. Within God's cosmic whole, we find individual selves with family and community identities. But for many in today's world of migration, exile, and rootlessness, the family circle will not be confined to the geographic

22. Martha C. Nussbaum, *Cultivating Humanity: A Classical Defense of Reform in Liberal Education* (Cambridge: Harvard University Press, 1997), 60.
23. Ibid.

community. And although one's local neighborhood is part of the national circle, in today's world of hybridity, creolization, and border crossings, many cultural neighborhoods have hazy geographic borders. The modern idea of the self, formed by individual and national identity, is being replaced by a textually constructed postmodern global self. *The Autobiography of Benjamin Franklin* at one time formed a united vision of American identity, but today's American as depicted in novels such as Jhumpa Lahiri's *The Namesake* inhabits multitudinous strands of being—political, cultural, ethnic, and religious.

I have come to believe that Christian literary scholars should be cosmopolitans in their reading, teaching, research, and scholarship, moving from the excessive nationalism often found in literary studies to study cultural particulars found across the globe. For Christians, the decline of the relatively short-lived phenomenon of the nation-state threatened by globalization may pose troubling issues with respect to peace and order, but in terms of allegiance and identity, the nation-state and American civil religion make many demands antithetical to Christian commitment. The American idolization of national identity often comes at the cost of authentic Christian commitment to love the neighbor, care for the earth, and worship the Triune God. Taking a global approach to literature allows us to balance our local identity—formed through our embodiment in a physical, social world—with a cosmopolitan identity endowed by our common creation in the image of God. I'm not suggesting that we eliminate our study of national identity and traditions—I currently teach more American than African literature, and my research program includes Emily Dickinson—but that we reframe that study in global terms, acknowledging the multiple monkey-ropes spinning out across the globe.

I no longer consider texts solely as national productions, but also examine the ways in which they participate in global culture. Although some texts are so closely tied to their local origin that they don't generate much meaning outside that context, many may be read one way in a national context and a different way in a global context. Such works participate in a "double conversation": "with their culture of origin and with the varied contexts into which they travel away from home."[24] Even texts produced in a drive to establish national identity have global components. For example, the "Young America" movement, exemplified by Irving's "Rip Van Winkle" or Emerson's "The American Scholar," is part of global nineteenth-century nationalism. The local process of constructing American identity is, in fact, intrinsically interrelated with global processes. For example, Emerson's much vaunted "Americanism," Lawrence Buell demonstrates, was thoroughly saturated with the Concord sage's extensive reading in East Asian sources.[25]

Nationalism also plays an important role in postcolonial literature, such as Ngũgĩ wa Thiong'o's A Grain of Wheat or Nelson Mandela's Long Walk to Freedom, assisting in the creation of emerging national identities. In Frantz Fanon's analysis, such narratives—as opposed to demeaning colonial narratives or nostalgic indigenous narratives—generate a genuine national culture. But Fanon hopes that postcolonial national identities will be fluid, "will make such a culture open to other cultures and . . . will enable it to influence and permeate other cultures."[26] Such efforts to form national identity through textual production and symbolic representation can participate in the double conversation of the local and the global, as when Chinua Achebe writes Things Fall Apart to show African readers "that we in Africa did not hear of culture for the first time from Europeans" as well as to reveal to European readers the complexity and humanity of indigenous Igbo culture.[27]

As worldwide connections multiply exponentially, globalization has radically reoriented the idea of neighborliness. Humanity's needs and "neighborliness" are rendered more apparent, are less easy to ignore, because of globalization. The respect for humanity grounded in the imago Dei and the love for neighbor stipulated by the Christian Scriptures are not limited to national, religious, or even geographic proximity. In the story of the good Samaritan, the neighbor is not

24. David Damrosch et al., eds., The Longman Anthology of World Literature (New York: Pearson Longman, 2004), 1:xix.
25. Lawrence Buell, Emerson (Cambridge, MA: Harvard University Press, 2004).
26. Frantz Fanon, The Wretched of the Earth, trans. Constance Farrington (New York: Grove Press, 1963), 245.
27. African Writers Talking, ed. Cosmo Pieterse and Dennis Duerden (New York: Africana, 1972), 7.

someone who lives next door, or goes to the same synagogue, or claims the same national identity: the neighbor is anyone in need. Theologian Gustavo Gutiérrez explains that by approaching the wounded man sprawled by the side of the road, the Samaritan *made* him his neighbor: "The neighbor is not [the one] whom I find in my path but rather [the one] in whose path I place myself, [the one] whom I approach and actively seek."[28] Thinking about faithful reading in the global community requires that we place ourselves in new paths, that we actively seek new neighbors.

Furthermore, in works of literature from unfamiliar traditions, we can delight in more expressions of human creativity. A Japanese haiku, a Zulu epic, and a Renaissance drama are all beautiful in extraordinarily different ways, but every burst of beauty points us to and reveals God. Catholic thinkers speak about this revelation in terms of the world's sacramental or iconic nature: God's self-revelation occurs not only through the sensible signs of the sacraments but also through all of sensible creation. In a sacramental worldview, "God is present in the visible, the tangible, the finite, and the historical,"[29] including the beauty of cultures other than our own. Protestant thought emphasizes how physical creation and human creations testify to the glory of God; in N. T. Wright's brilliant description, beauty "is an echo of a voice, not the voice itself."[30] However, our pleasure in a well-crafted plot, a vivid character, or an apt phrase is not merely a Platonic shadow of ideal Beauty, but something real and good in itself, however incomplete and unrestored, a common-grace blessing. Reading global literature grants us access to more beauty and thus expands our knowledge and experience of God.

For Western Christians, global reading can also enlarge our limited understanding of God and the Christian story. Since humans were created as social and cultural beings, we can only apprehend the Christian kerygma within a particular historical context—or, as Calvin puts it, God lovingly adjusts to speak in ways that humans can understand.

28. Quoted in Robert McAfee Brown, *Unexpected News: Reading the Bible with Third World Eyes* (Louisville: Westminster John Knox, 1984), 112.

29. Robert McBrien, *Catholicism* (New York: Harper Collins, 1994), 10.

30. N. T. Wright, *Simply Christian: Why Christianity Makes Sense* (San Francisco: HarperSanFrancisco, 2006), 43.

We access the infinite only through cultural particulars. The mystery of the incarnation affirms that human cultural particularity is the means by which God is revealed. God became a particular Jewish man in order to reveal God's self to us. That's not to say that God is either Jewish or a man. However, human selfishness and tendency toward idolatry often induce us to assume that our culturally rooted understanding is the complete transcendent truth (ironically, also one of the insights of the postmodern project). The growth of world Christianity increases the number of cultural angles on Christian truth available for us to dialogue with, triangulate from, and with which to recognize our myopia.

Within global cultures, the bread and butter of literary texts—language, narratives, images, and metaphors—reveal new visions of Christianity and faith, as the experiences of Father Vincent J. Donovan demonstrate. Sent to work among the Masai in the 1960s, Father Donovan was painfully aware of previous destructive missionary impositions of Western customs and culture, so he decided not to affiliate himself with a mission school or hospital, but rather to live among the Masai and attempt to communicate the gospel message without cultural trappings. However, he soon realized that the only way to articulate the meaning of salvation was within a cultural context. He writes, "As I began to ponder the evangelization of the Masai, I had to realize that God enables a people, any people, to reach salvation through their culture and . . . traditions. . . . I had no right to disrupt this body of customs, of traditions. It was the way of salvation for these people, their way to God."[31] Donovan began listening to Masai views of the gospel, which not only made his missionary work more successful but also opened up his faith in new ways.

Once Father Donovan was talking with a Masai elder:

> He said for a man really to believe is like a lion going after its prey. His nose and eyes and ears pick up the prey. His legs give him the speed to catch it. All the power of his body is involved in the terrible death leap and single blow to the neck with the front paw, the blow that actually

31. Vincent J. Donovan, *Christianity Rediscovered*, 2nd ed. (Maryknoll, NY: Orbis, 1978), 30.

kills. And as the animal goes down, the lion envelops it in his arms . . .
pulls it to himself, and makes it part of himself. This is the way a lion
kills. This is the way a man believes. This is what faith is.[32]

Father Donovan was amazed at the total commitment and spiritual
hunger embodied in this analogy, but the elder then adds, "We have
not searched for him. He has searched for us. He has searched us out
and found us. All the time we think we are the lion. In the end, the
lion is God."[33] Father Donovan's experience among the Masai was,
he says in the title of his book, "Christianity rediscovered."

Just as Dante in medieval Italy or Milton in Restoration England
relayed the Christian story in their own cultural images, so today
rural African women compose songs on their way home after hearing
a sermon, producing new forms of oral literature that translate the
Christian message. African texts have envisioned Christ as an anti-
apartheid prophet in *Woza Albert!* and as a suffering child in Uwem
Akpan's *Say You're One of Them*, giving us new views of the son
of God and man. All such cultural representations of God, Jesus,
Christianity, and salvation have both insights and shortcomings that
require discernment; the dialogue facilitated by cosmopolitan reading
will reveal both cultural limits and cultural contributions.

Another contribution of world literature is to provide fresh perspectives on the emerging church in the global South, critiquing as well
as celebrating its achievements. Literary works often contain critical
and nuanced representations demonstrating that the "triumph" of
Christianity in the global South is not always a "triumph" but also
may have troubling components, just as the earlier spread of Christendom had. Christian-Muslim conflicts, abusive attitudes toward
women and homosexuals, the rejection of historical denominationalist
Christianity, tensions between Western medicine and faith healing,
and the excesses of the health-and-wealth gospel are all represented
and explored in African literature today.

Reading as a Christian cosmopolitan brings me into different
worlds. It allows me to meet remote cousins who take the invisible
links that connect people far more seriously than most of my American

32. Ibid., 63.
33. Ibid.

neighbors. Global literature has given me glimpses of the sorrows of African AIDS orphans, for whom I lament. It has blessed me with fresh conceptions of the beauty of proverbs, and unfamiliar ways to think about family, love, gratitude, and forgiveness. Reading, teaching, and writing in a spirit of Christian cosmopolitanism gives me new ways to understand, love, and delight in both God and my neighbor.

Adichie's Fiction and Global Christianity

That's why, in addition to Emily Dickinson, I've also been working on a contemporary Nigerian writer named Chimamanda Ngozi Adichie, who has been widely celebrated as one of the most significant new global voices in African literature. Her first novel, *Purple Hibiscus* (2003), won the Commonwealth Writers' Prize, and her second, *Half of a Yellow Sun* (2006), took the Orange Prize for Fiction, one of the United Kingdom's most prestigious literary awards. Adichie was awarded a 2008 MacArthur Foundation "Genius Grant" Fellowship, and in 2009 published a short-story collection, *The Thing around Your Neck*. Her third novel, *Americanah*, was published in the spring of 2013.

Adichie's lyrically written fiction frequently depicts the competing religious realities that are central to contemporary Nigerian life. Raised as a Catholic, Adichie explains, "I am fascinated by the power of religion. . . . I think religion will probably feature in some way in everything I write—it, and the idea of faith itself, is something that I question, grapple with, almost daily."[34] *The Thing around Your Neck* contains twelve absorbing stories revolving around questions of identity in an era of globalization, including the impact of religion. Faith is a central part of global citizenship, and Adichie's fiction helps us to recognize the truths and the lies, the connections and the divisions, created by this fact. The "things" hanging around all of our necks are complicated strands of social, cultural, religious, and historical roots that gradually weave into the cord of one's self.

34. Ike Anya, "In the Footsteps of Achebe: Enter Chimamanda Ngozi Adichie," Africanwriter.com, http://www.africanwriter.com/in-the-footsteps-of-achebe-enter-chimamanda-ngozi-adichie/.

In one memorable story called "The Shivering," Adichie contrasts
the experiences of a Princeton graduate student who is the daughter
of a "big man" from Lagos, with that of a less-educated village man
who is facing deportation from the United States because his visa
has expired. Ukamaka and Chinedu meet when a plane crashes in
Nigeria, and he knocks on her apartment door while she is anxiously
monitoring the internet for news. "I am Nigerian," he announces. "I
live on the third floor. I came so that we can pray about what is hap-
pening in our country."[35] A Catholic who is struggling with her faith,
Ukamaka is wary of this uber-religious stranger, but Chinedu takes
her hand, and "he prayed in that particularly Nigerian Pentecostal
way that made her uneasy: he covered things with the blood of Jesus,
he bound up demons and cast them in the sea, he battled evil spirits."[36]
As the prayer grows more loudly fervent, Ukamaka's skepticism also
swells, but then the story takes an unexpected turn:

> She felt herself start to shiver, an involuntary quivering of her whole
> body. Was it God? Once, years ago when she was a teenager who me-
> ticulously said the rosary every morning, words she did not understand
> had burst out of her mouth as she knelt by the scratchy wooden frame
> of her bed. It had lasted a mere second, that outpouring of incom-
> prehensive words in the middle of a Hail Mary, but she had truly . . .
> felt terrified and sure that the white-cool feeling that enveloped her
> was God. [Her boyfriend] said she had created the experience herself.
> But how could I have? She had asked. How could I create something
> I did not even want?[37]

As the story unfolds, Ukamaka probes what it means to "have faith"
and to love, in conversation with both the conservative Chinedu and
a liberal Catholic priest. These discussions eventually prompt her to
move beyond her self-absorption and petty obsession with her former
boyfriend to become a genuine friend to Chinedu, who then reveals
his own struggle with being an African, a Christian, and a gay man.
No facile resolution occurs, but the story concludes with Chinedu

35. Chimamanda Ngozi Adichie, "The Shivering," in *The Thing around Your Neck* (New York: Knopf, 2009), 143.
36. Ibid.
37. Ibid., 144.

attending mass with Ukamaka, the two laughing joyously together as they share a pew with a woman and baby, who suggest hope. The final lines celebrate the Christian community formed by baptism, despite cultural differences:

> It was one of those Sundays when the priest blessed the congregation with holy water at the beginning of Mass, and Father Patrick was walking up and down, flicking water on the people with something that looked like a big saltshaker. Ukamaka watched him and thought how much more subdued Catholic Masses were in America; how in Nigeria it would have been a vibrant green branch from a mango tree that the priest would dip in a bucket of holy water held by a hurrying, sweating, Mass-server; how he would have stridden up and down, splashing and swirling, holy water raining down; how the people would have been drenched; and how, smiling and making the sign of the cross, they would have felt blessed.[38]

Adichie's fiction superbly captures global Christianity, with attention to the local and the universal as well as the gifts and challenges of Christian faith within the monkey-ropes of human existence.

38. Ibid., 166.

❖ 6 ❖

Epilogue

The *Pequod* sinks, relentlessly drawing its cosmopolitan crew into a watery vortex, but Ishmael survives, testifying in his epilogue, "And I only am escaped alone to tell thee." The final word of *Moby-Dick* is *orphan*. "Only," "alone," "to," "orphan"—the assonance evokes woe as Melville laments the loss of human community. In contrast, I have learned to recognize and love the multiple communities that buoy me up—from my Lynden roots, to Westmont's evangelicalism, to Emory's intellectual community, to Calvin's Reformed mind, to SPU's Wesleyan warmth, to the sustaining language of the Book of Common Prayer.

I have been held in love by God and God's people throughout my life, even when unexpected waves enveloped me and I was gasping for air. Painful events, such as my experience with cancer and an unwanted and emotionally draining divorce in 2008, gave me a minor taste of the suffering and lamentation found in the literary texts that I studied, while, at the same time, they gently revealed the deep mysteries of steadfast love and grace.

I continue to believe in the centrality of an intellectual approach to Christian education and scholarship, but events over the past three decades of my life have taught me how my heart complements my head and how my childish individual delight in literature is enhanced by and located in human community. I have learned that a human being's perspectival stance goes beyond philosophical and theological commitments and is formed by experience, gender, ethnic identity, socioeconomic class, geographical location, and other subject-positions. I gradually began to grasp that my reading of literature was both enhanced and limited by my position as a white, American, Christian woman, and I needed other perspectives in order to see behind and beyond myself.

The philosopher Charles Taylor wonderfully describes the kind of human unity that is formed through such a process: "Redemption-Incarnation brings reconciliation, a kind of oneness. This is the oneness of diverse beings who come to see that they cannot attain wholeness alone, that their complementarity is essential, rather than of beings who come to accept that they are ultimately identical."[1] In my academic voyage, I have learned to listen to the diverse but complementary voices that form humanity and to attend to the delight and the sorrow, the aesthetic achievements and the cultural insight, such voices evoked.

As a Reformed Christian, I have also learned much from other theological voices. I have visited many branches of the Christian family tree at SPU, in my work for the CCCU, my participation in the national Lilly Programs for Theological Education, and, most recently, my service as SPU's representative to the Lilly Fellows Program in Humanities and the Arts (LFP). Based at Valparaiso University, the LFP seeks to strengthen the quality and shape the character of church-related institutions of higher learning in the twenty-first century, and LFP schools include Catholic, Lutheran, mainline denominational, and evangelical institutions, with a variety of ways of maintaining their religious character. As a mentor with the LFP Graduate Fellows Program, working with Professor Patrick Byrne from Boston College, I have grown to appreciate the wisdom found in the Roman Catholic tradition. With our sixteen graduate students, we spent one semester studying the topic "Protestants and Catholics in Conversation," and we all grew to understand each other better. I now believe that

1. Charles Taylor, *A Catholic Modernity? Charles Taylor's Marianist Award Lecture*, ed. James L. Heft (New York: Oxford University Press, 1999), 14.

the Catholic and Anglican respect for the sacramental nature of the world and the formative power of liturgical worship enhance Christian learning and scholarship. I believe that the Anabaptist prophetic commitment to social action enhances Christian learning and scholarship. And, from my Wesleyan colleagues at SPU, I have learned how God's healing love and abundant grace enhance Christian learning and scholarship.

My views of Christian higher education and the relationship of Christianity and culture have also evolved as I've realized that despite the central truths of Christian orthodoxy, C. S. Lewis's "mere Christianity" or N. T. Wright's "simply Christian" are articulated through strikingly different language, images, practices, and cultures throughout time and history. There is no one "Christian worldview" accessible to anyone but God; instead, we have multiple historical and cultural manifestations of God's eternal truth, many variations on the central melody of creation and salvation that we must constantly retune and transpose.

Similarly, H. Richard Niebuhr's typology of Christ and culture—Christ against culture, Christ of culture, Christ above culture, Christ and culture in paradox, and Christ transforming culture—which once helped me grasp different intellectual approaches to learning, is too simplistic. As Taylor's work demonstrates, "in modern, secularist culture there are mingled together both authentic developments of the gospel, of an incarnational mode of life, and also a closing off to God that negates the gospel."[2] The modern affirmation of ordinary human life, the concern for human rights, and a commitment to benevolence and justice, Taylor argues, originate in the gospel, but modernity has closed the door on the transcendent, including the mysteries of suffering and self-sacrificial love, the reality of human evil, and the ontological basis for morality. "Culture" is not monolithically Christian or non-Christian, and it takes many divergent forms across the globe.

As a teacher, then, I've moved beyond identifying presuppositions and worldviews (although I still do this to a certain degree) to encourage students to ruminate on the unfolding development of their

2. Ibid., 16.

narrative identity within God's metanarrative; to study an idea or thing carefully and honestly, determining both its strengths and weaknesses; to celebrate God's truth and beauty no matter where it is found; and to be constantly vigilant to learn about suffering, injustice, and oppression.

I believe that the decisions we make about scholarly projects or curricular structures should be decisions about the way in which we might, through our work as scholars and teachers, contribute to the coming of shalom and the flourishing of all God's people. These decisions should be vocational rather than strictly professional. In an era when research topics are chosen for their market value and junior faculty are often intent on publishing solely for publishing's sake, Christian scholars should think in terms of calling and service. Emerging scholars should prayerfully consider studying Chinese or Spanish or Xhosa or texts from the global South and East. Similarly, we should introduce our undergraduate students to literature beyond the Western canon and help them to read that canon in new ways in order to become better neighbors in today's global world.

Christian literary scholars, I believe, should say both yes and no to our discipline. We should neither completely nor uncritically adopt new theories and ways of reading, but we should also not worry about creating a different or unique school of "Christian criticism." Rather, we should practice faithful scholarship in obedience to God. We need to stay up to date in our discipline and active in professional organizations, speaking both to the church and to the secular academy. Faithful scholarship, to my way of thinking, remains a vital part of the vocation of a Christian college professor and should not be neglected, even in teaching institutions. We need to lodge our professorial work thoughtfully in our theology and ground our life fundamentally in Christian formative practices, asking sometimes neglected questions, celebrating beauty and truth wherever it may be found, and rejoicing in the diversity of tribe and nation and culture that will ultimately be reconciled in the peaceful kingdom of the new earth.

Seattle
All Saints' Day, 2012

Index

Abrams, M. H., 39
Achebe, Chinua, 73–74, 76–77, 84–85, 120
Adichie, Chimamanda Ngozi, 124–26
Africa
  and Christianity, 114–16, 122–26
  history of, 83, 84
  See also African literature; Nigeria; postcolonialism; South Africa
African American literature
  and criticism, 43, 63, 78
African literature
  and Christianity, 82, 84, 93–96, 124–26
  difficulties publishing, 100, 101–4
  and globalization, 110, 114, 123–24, 126
  study of, 2, 78, 82–87, 106, 110, 115–16
  See also South African literature
Age of Iron (Coetzee), 70
Akpan, Uwem, 123
All We're Meant to Be (Scanzoni and Hardesty), 45
Americanah (Adichie), 124
American Literature (journal), 52
amnesty, and confession, 96, 98–99
Amnesty International, 95, 117
Anabaptist social action, 129
Andalusia, 31
Anna Karenina (Tolstoy), 8
apartheid, 48–49, 51, 69–70, 87, 92–93, 95–96, 102–3, 123. *See also* South Africa
Armstrong, Neil, 10

Arnold, Matthew, 58, 61
Art in Action: Toward a Christian Aesthetic (Wolterstorff), 58, 66
Auden, W. H., 35
Austen, Jane, 63
Autobiography of Benjamin Franklin, The, 119

Bâ, Mariama, 85
Bakhtin, Mikhail, 74–75, 90–91, 102
Barcus, James, 53–54
Barrington College, 54
Baylor University, 53, 54
Baym, Nina, 44
beauty, 121
Bell, Gloria, 54
Bible
  on creation, 58–59
  and feminism, 42, 44–46
  and justice, 73
  and literature, 58
Biko, Steve, 93
bildungsroman, African, 86
Bloom, Allan, 62, 63
Boston College, 128
Bratt, James D., 5n5, 6–7, 55
Breytenbach, Breyten, 92
Brink, Andre, 100
Brooks, Cleanth, 34
Buell, Lawrence, 120
Byrne, Patrick, 128

Calvin, John, 49, 56, 121
Calvin Center for Christian Scholarship, 65
Calvin College, 55–57, 64, 65, 77–79, 106–7
  faculty of, 23, 54–55
  Lynden connection with, 12, 16

scholarship at, 65, 88
Calvinism
  of Dutch American communities, 4, 55–57
  and neo-Calvinism, 49, 56, 62, 64, 73, 77
  progressive and traditionalist, 55–57
  on sanctification and original sin, 109
  See also Reformed tradition
canon, literary, 34–35, 42–44, 61–64, 76, 78, 105, 130
Cary, Joyce, 84
catechetical instruction, 6, 11, 107
Chaucer, Geoffrey, 33, 63
Chicago, University of, 117
Christ
  and culture (Niebuhr), 129
  as sovereign, 55
  See also Jesus
Christian colleges, 18, 21–22, 41, 46–47, 53–54, 58, 61, 87–88, 105, 107–10, 116, 129–30
Christianity
  and African literature, 82, 84, 93–96, 110, 114, 116, 123–26
  and cosmopolitanism, 117–19, 123–24
  and culture, 23–24, 58–60, 62, 114–15, 121–23, 129
  and globalization, 110–11, 114–16, 119, 122–26, 130
  and literary scholars, 54, 57–64, 66, 119, 130
  and postcolonial literature, 72–73
  and scholarship, 107–9, 127–29
  as world-formative, 49–50

131